Copyright © 2017 Daniel Gerber

All rights reserved. No part of this book may be reproduced
or used in any manner without the prior written permission of the
copyright owner,
except for the use of brief quotations in a book review.

Paperback: 978-0-692-95710-3
Lightning Source LLC, 14 Ingram Blvd
La Vergne, TN 37086

www.IngramSpark.com

True Faith
A philosophy on faith and religion
By: Daniel Gerber

In amid the fighting and turmoil,
the struggle and shouting and gnashing teeth
a moment is taken, where the roar is soft and silent
and the torrent of wind and debris dies down.
I find comfort there, as I take a breath of creation
and allow myself to be in God's presence for a change.
Like a mother, I feel her come to me full of understanding
Like a lover, she holds me, her soft hand upon my face
A smell of soft lilac as I lay beside her
and she whispers to me "it's okay."
She holds me as long as I desire, and does not change.
No tear is judged, not a word is spoken
and for a time the broken screaming of the world
is no more than the whispering of the breeze.

Contents

Foreword	i
Definitions	v

The Search For A True Faith

Faith	1
Faith Vs Religion	3
The Point Of Faith/Belief	8
True Faith	12
God	14
God vs. other worship	14
God Does Not Micromanage	15
In the Absence of God	18
Bigotry	26
The Blind Men and the Elephant	26
The Priest and the Preacher	28
The Bigot	33
Ouroboros	39

Foundational Principles

The Path	45
Simple Truths	49
Fate vs. Drive	54
Humanity's Knowledge	65
Non-believers	74
Prayer	78
Right and Wrong	83
Good vs. Evil	84
Qualifying Evil	93
The Ten Sins	96
Altruism	140
Neither Good or Evil	168
The Important Question	178
In Conclusion	182
About the Author	182
Sources	187

Foreword

Before I begin, I would like to make something perfectly clear. This work is not a new religion, or some new age philosophy. It is not meant as an attack on any faith or religion or culture. The purpose of this writing is to stimulate the mind toward the development of faith, encourage the search for truth, and empower the reader to fight against bigotry through reason and understanding.

This work is written about major topics within the purview of religious writing as well as the nature of intolerant behavior. I began writing it because there is a gap in The United States of America between those who belong to a specific religion and those who do not believe in God at all. That gap is filled with people who do not fall into a religion but still believe in God. Without an established group of people to identify with, the development of faith is significantly more challenging without great contemplation and a lot of people simply do not spend time developing their faith. This writing serves to give those people a place to start and hopefully those without a defined faith can construct a reasonable and good faith using some of the concepts in this book without needing to rely on the trappings of any one religion.

To get the most out of this writing, I encourage you to merely read and consider, not assume that these contents are facts. Though much of the reasoning and beliefs in this book are based on the observation of truth, many of the points within could be argued and should be looked at with a skeptical mind so as to better discern the logic within the topics discussed and consider whether or not they hold true and are reasonable from your own perspective.

So far, as humanity continues to advance and people strive to make sense of the universe, (and there is a awful lot to make sense of) religion has managed to estrange itself from its foundation. The essence of faith has managed to become separated from logic and truth. Going back to Christianity, and its predecessor Judaism, there's a large disconnect between the things taught and written and the things currently practiced. As science, philosophy, technology and society have evolved, religions every now and again have modified themselves in order to stay relevant, updating dogma so it can mesh with current trends in science and philosophy. These transitions tend to be clunky and unsatisfactory. Ideas like "When Moses did this" and "the pharaoh did that" or "back then such and such, and it still applies today" often cease to fit into our world. Human nature is the same today as it was thousands of years ago but some messages have less to do with human nature and more to do with needs of the times and erroneous perceptions of the era in which they arose. It's like trying to mash a puzzle piece in the wrong place. Even though the piece almost sort of fits, in spite of the colors not matching, people keep trying to say "see, the puzzle still works". That disconnect, that inability to mesh incongruous thoughts, leads to the downfall of a religion over time. People have proven adept at recognizing incongruous pieces, and as such with our current recorded history we know that we have transitioned from one belief to another over the centuries in the search for a concrete truth. So, instead of trying to apply modern ways of thinking to make an outdated machine work, it seems pertinent to use a modern way of thinking to redefine our core of beliefs. Does it not seem possible that the building blocks we've used for so long to build our faith on are insufficient? Or have we merely forgotten what a true faith is?

  It can be argued that the largest plague on humanity's well being is religion. I do not mean a belief in a higher power or the teachings of a particular religion.

After all, most religions preach tolerance and peace. I mean that religion, a structured organization of common faith beliefs, has been at the root of wars, death, famine, suffering, depression and a lot of other things that many of us wish to eradicate. Some of these afflictions occur on an individual level such as grief, guilt, alienation, low self-esteem, etc. These manifest in people who cannot make sense of their beliefs, or in those who believe in a religion taught to them by others, causing them to fall into ignorance with beliefs and practices that do not make logical sense and do not serve the greater good. It is sobering to think that a belief in a benevolent deific power should have such a harmful effect on people. So why does it?

Every religion on this planet has its problems. Every one has its good sides and its bad. And none of them are perfect. Every religion seems to have an insufficient definition of beliefs. If a religion is truly worth pursuit, wouldn't the majority of humanity flock to it? If that is the case then it seems to me that it is not a fault within any specific religion, but rather the foundation that our faiths are built upon that cause the them to fall short.

In other words, if you try to construct a building on a stone foundation, and every building you create has massive flaws and structurally needs to be updated and retrofitted to continue to stand, then perhaps it is not the building itself you should be worried about, but the foundation it rests upon. You cannot build a sound structure on an unsound foundation. Christ knew that, carpenters know that, yet we continue to have problems. If we're going to form a faith truly worth having then we must consider the possibility that our foundations must be rethought. That's not to say that the entire foundation is poorly built, but rather that some parts and pieces may be ill-formed or structurally unsound.

While we are often victims of our own emotions,

humanity is logical in nature. We seek to find order and meaning in everything. That is the foundation of science. Why then, should we not do so with religion? I doubt very much that God wants us to be confused about our lives and the world around us. The world follows logical patterns. If there is a great creator of all things, and everything around us follows logical progression, why should our faith in that great creator be any less logical.

Simply put, if it doesn't make logical sense, rethink it. We should strive for a faith that makes sense, even if it seems difficult if not impossible to attain. A lot of people forswear religion simply because it does not make sense. I have heard many times that religion and science are incompatible. It is time that we change that perception.

As mentioned before, this work is not about creating a new religion, nor undoing religions already in existence. Firstly, and most importantly, the intent of this work is to breed tolerance for other beliefs and encourage people to forgo bigotry in the name of truth. Through sound reason and by cultivating a longing for truth, we can breed tolerance and acceptance for beliefs other than our own. Secondly, the goal is to promote your thoughts and help you forge a logical and reasonable foundation of faith, to provide yourself with the necessary blocks of belief to build upon as each of us strives to find meaning in a world too immense and immeasurable for any one of us to fully comprehend.

Definitions

I don't know about you, but I have heard more heated arguments concerning religion than I can count, and certainly more than I care for. The biggest problem with those kinds of arguments is that every one of us has our own perspective of religious belief. Misconceptions are sure to arise when discussing spiritual belief, so it is all the more important to ensure that a common understanding is established before further discussion takes place. People have different definitions of certain concepts, and one of the reasons people have such a hard time holding constructive conversations about faith beliefs is that everyone views the terms of the conversation differently. To help mitigate that problem, here are the terms most important to our discussion. The following definitions will be used to serve as a premise for the contents of this book.

God:
As I use God in this document, I am referring to the higher power and/or the creator of the universe, not necessarily the God of any specific religion. God could mean both a singular entity or God could stand for a pantheon. Since a pantheon, though consisting of multiple entities, is defined as a singular entity in itself consisting of many parts, I will denote it as singular by referring to it as God. I could say Allah, or Hashem, or countless other names for the same thing, but God only has three letters, and lets face it, it's just less of a mouth full to say. Perhaps it is an oversimplification but consider this: In Taoist philosophy, Lao-Tzu's teachings say that "the name that can be named is not the eternal Name." (Lao Tzu 1) So, no matter what we decide to call God, God's name cannot be named. However, if we're going to have this discussion we have to have some sort of word to use in order to discuss it.

In this way, naming the creator God, I seek only the means to communicate precisely that: The creator of all things is God.

"There was something formless and perfect before the universe was born. It is serene. Empty. Solitary. Unchanging. Infinite. Eternally present. It is the mother of the universe. For lack of a better name, I call it the Tao." (Lao Tzu 25)

Additionally, Another way to view God is not as an entity such as a person or place, but as the force that governs all. Defining God as a person or place restricts God to what is easiest for us to imagine. That is necessary for some in order to wrap our minds around the concept but not necessarily what is true. Perhaps God is a bit of both; Force and Creator. We see God as that which governs the universe regardless of shape and form, so a governing force makes sense.

In another way, God is not an entity, but a reason. If science is the expression of How and When and What and Where the universe works, God perhaps is the expression of Why.

It is the conceptual nature of God that gives rise to controversy among people with differing viewpoints. That is why defining God is so critical to holding constructive conversations. There is, however, a true nature of the world and many believe it includes a higher power. Intelligent design, creationism and a whole world of ideas about how and why the universe exists spawn from that belief. God is an important facet of faith and religion, and for many of us its presence or absence says a great deal to us about the nature of existence and the reason we are here.

Religion:

Religion is defined as a set of beliefs concerning the cause, nature, and purpose of the universe, usually involving devotional and ritual observances, and often containing a moral code governing the conduct of human affairs. Religion is a set of beliefs and practices generally agreed upon by a number of persons or sects and adhered to by a body of people. (Dictionary.com, Religion) Without a large number of people believing in the same thing, a belief is not a religion.

Religion can also be defined as ritual observance of faith.

Faith:

An overwhelming belief in something without proof to confirm it or to condemn it. Also sometimes to be noted as a system of religious belief. (Dictionary.com, faith)

We should note that while Religion and Faith are both similar, they are not the same. Faith requires belief while religion requires a body of people. This distinction is core to our discussion because faith and religion have different effects within our society. To help differentiate between the two for our conversation, imagine a religion complete with church, holidays, rituals, and a system of hierarchy such that you might find in a heavily structured religion with priests, bishops, cardinals and popes. For faith, imagine a person or small group of people who have a belief but do not partake in any of the characteristics noted above for religion.

With these definitions in mind we can discuss faith and religion with a common understanding in the hopes that there can be some sort of productivity to our conversation

The Search For A True Faith

Faith

"... What are the three kinds of faith? They are, first, sincere faith; second, deep faith; and third, the faith that seeks birth there (in heaven) by transferring one's merit." (Kyokai 92)

Faith: An overwhelming belief in something without proof to confirm it or to condemn it. Also sometimes to be noted as a system of religious belief. (Dictionary.com, faith)

Its definition as a system of religious belief seems secondary to the first definition. All religions hold to a belief. A simple truth: Faith is important to those who keep it. Faith forms a core that human beings cling to and live by. Mankind is most likely to act according to the facets of their belief than for any other reason. Not just in religion, or spirituality, but in everyday life.

For example, if a person believes that they are going to get fired from their job, their emotional attitude when going to work that day will be different than if they did not believe they were going to be fired. While in this example they have no proof of their termination it affects how they hold themselves and how they behave. That person might try even harder to do a good job at work that day if they believe it will help them hold their position. They might also do an even worse job if they believe that their effort is pointless and see no reason to perform their duties well. Their choice in how to behave might also be connected to their beliefs. A person who doesn't believe their job is worth keeping might very well give up and do a poor job until they are terminated. For a person who believes in upholding their dignity and striving hard to do well in everything they do, they might be inclined to do a good job in spite of their potential termination. Whatever the circumstances, humankind acts according to their beliefs, even if there is no concrete proof that what they believe is true.

It is striking to note that throughout history humankind habitually comes to a spiritual or deific faith especially in times of crisis. Faith has been around since the dawn of mankind. It seems we are doomed to return to it for several reasons. The first reason is the search for the truth in the absence of explanation. Before mankind understood science and medicine, illness was ascribed to spirits and the wrath of the gods. Nobody understood the reason behind the malady and so its was taken in faith.

The search for truth in the absence of explanation is where we seek to understand the origin of existence. We want to know how and why we got here. Unfortunately, science can only take us as far as our comprehension allows. Any further than that, and we have to take the explanation of existence on faith.

The second reason we turn to faith is for a sense of support in our daily lives when things go wrong. When we are alone and there's no one to turn to, loneliness sets in and we seek comfort from a presence of some kind. As social creatures, it is understandable. We seek to survive with others as it is in our nature. We have difficulties surviving alone. We seek God as a means of companionship.

The third reason seems all the more important than the other two for it comes to those who seek a reason for being. The first reason for faith is the simple question "How?" This is the basis of science. The second reason is the question "who?" or "with whom?". (Understandably not the most important question, but viable all the same.) We want to know who we are and who we are with. The third reason for faith is the strongest question: Why? This query is the basis of existentialism, which we will discuss later. Mankind seeks to know why we are here, why we live and die, why we suffer and why we love. It is a ponderous question that the other two reasons for faith do not approach.   Strangely, not everyone asks the question "why?", and even fewer strive to find a satisfying answer. However, since the nature of existence denies us a straightforward answer, the question of "why?" falls into faith. We have a belief as to why we are here, why there is a here that we are within, yet we do not have proof to support those beliefs.

If we don't have proof, what do we have? We have faith. Some might view faith as a flaw, defying reason and logic, but in many ways it is one of our greatest strengths. Faith enables us to do the right thing, to be stronger than we might otherwise be and to press onward when things may seem hopeless. Faith is what drives us, and is perhaps the most important thing in any person's life. Without it, we are lost.

Faith Vs Religion

Religion is defined as a set of beliefs concerning the cause, nature, and purpose of the universe, usually involving devotional and ritual observances, and often containing a moral code governing the conduct of human affairs. Religion is a set of beliefs and practices generally agreed upon by a number of persons or sects and adhered to by a body of people. (Dictionary.com, Religion)

It is important to note that by this definition, a body of people is required. Some of the pitfalls of religion occur due to the presence of that body of people which we will discuss later.

Religion can also be defined as a ritual observance of faith. This latter definition, though simplistic, does not include the need for a body of people, and in this sense is a more structured approach to faith. Without the inclusion of a body of people, religion is only as corruptible as the one who observes it.

So, does a person need religion?

The answer is no.

In the the United States of America in 2014 a survey was conducted by Time Magazine which concluded that about twenty three percent of the population did not affiliate themselves with a religion. (Nov 3rd, 2016) Though it is helpful to have others to rely on we are not a mentally collective people. A person does not think someone else's thoughts. They think their own. We are, however, a socially collective people.

Like many things, there are strong points to religion. A community with common beliefs can be a safe haven during hard times and a good influence for a person's social development. However, a spiritual journey is exactly that; a journey. It's not a book to be handed over and obtained. It is not a ritual that is carried out and then considered complete. A spiritual journey has a place it starts, and a destination it seeks to reach.

Within the context of social religion, a person should not be blinded by what they are told, but discover for themselves what they can. Religion hands out dogma and prepared verses, but not necessarily truth. That is one of the great flaws with religious writings. Prepared verses do not always inspire everyone who hears and often the intent of those verses can become lost. It would be unreasonable to say that you have reached the summit of a mountain simply because someone told you what it was like and how to get there when you yourself had never been to that summit. Faith is a path to be traveled to discern truth through the self's journey, not through the journey of others.

If a religion tells us something is important then we should take the time to discover if it rings true or not, either through experience or contemplation, and whether or not it accomplishes the good that it should. If truth follows the message given us by our religion, that is wonderful. We need to hang on to that. If not, we should take the time to find the truth of the message for ourselves. In that way we do not open ourselves to the misconceptions of others.

I see a lot of people who take the words of others on faith and don't take the time to discover the truth on their own. This method of spiritual pursuit is susceptible to the agendas and ignorance of others, as well as fears and misgivings. That kind of blind following is why religious wars are even possible in spite of many religions delivering messages of peace and tolerance, and surely that cannot be a good thing.

"Accursed is the man who trusts in people and makes mortals his strength, and turns his heart away from Hashem."
(Stone Edition Chumash, The Haftaros Bechukosai 17, 5)

It is through the journey that we gain faith and discover truth. Surely if you are striving to serve God and walk in his ways, God will not lead you astray.

That being said, should we say that all religion is bad? No. Of course not. Though perhaps we would be a more peaceable people if we didn't have such a varied topic to squabble over, such is not the point of this writing. As I said, religion has its good points. The concern over the presence of religion is the damage religion is capable of because it is made up of a body of people. Religion is vulnerable to the same things a person is vulnerable to. Religion can be corrupted, just as man can be corrupted. We are fallible. It's human nature. There's nothing wrong with that, that's just how it is. We need simply be aware of it, and humble enough to recognize that we could be wrong and that we are capable of making mistakes. Religion can hurt and cause harm in the name of "what is good". Many wars have been started based on religious differences or beliefs (even in spite of the belief that one should not kill another). That speaks great volumes to the flaws of religion. It is only in a structured social religion that we can grow to fight religious wars. Without the structure of religion, the influence of flawed individuals only goes as far as one person's influence. A religious leader with thousands of followers could potentially have a "holy army" of thousands. An individual practicing a faith only has influence over the people connected to their life, more than likely only a hundred or less, and probably only a fraction of those people would be committed to the beliefs of that individual. An army of twenty cannot do nearly as much damage as an army of thousands. Thus, a less structured faith practice has less potential to do harm.

    The more complex a thing is, the more potential for its systemic failure or corruption. Often, in religious structures, there is a hierarchy, and those at the top have the most authority for what is "the message of god to give down to the people". All it takes is one opinion, one thought that is tempered not by reason or righteousness, but by any number of destructive tendencies, to taint and twist the faith of people who listen and take heed. If those at the top of a hierarchy fail to live by the ideals they teach, those ideals are not likely to be lived by those at the bottom of the hierarchy. That is why blindly following a religion and taking what is spoken or written as empirical fact is such a dangerous thing to do. If the head of a church says that Muslims are sinners and enemies of God, for example, there will be many who believe it. What will the result of that kind of combativeness be? I have a hard time imagining that it would be anything good. That is why it is imperative to see things as they are and not blindly trust the beliefs of others. People lie. People embellish. Sometimes people put things into a perspective that doesn't seem so bad in order to serve personal desires. We do it out of fear, out of love, out of jealousy, pride or for any number of other reasons. It is a fatal flaw and when placed in a structured practice of faith it can have catastrophic effects. The events over the last two thousand plus years are proof enough of that. You needn't look far to find prime examples of poor leadership and blind followers. Just remember that devoting your life to God is not the same to devoting your life to a religion, nor is it the same thing as devoting your life to a church. There are many instances where these distinctions may overlap, but we should never lose sight that they are different devotions and the latter two have a greater potential to lead a person astray.

  People who follow others are subject to the faults of their leaders. Instead of teaching people to follow, or teaching people to lead others, to prevent the destruction brought about by religion people must be taught to lead themselves. There is a saying that instead of trying to carpet the entire world, we should learn to wear shoes. If we seek to cultivate people like sheep, as the Christian metaphor would go, those sheep will follow the other sheep even so far as off the edge of a cliff and then there will be few who remain.

  God gave men eyes with which to see, a mind to reason, and a body to act. It is a shame to waste those gifts by relying on the sight and reason of others. Remember: humans are imperfect. It is better to seek God and follow his directions, than to follow a man who seeks god, for, like yourself, his judgment is imperfect, and he may stumble.

  Many people go to church not for religion, but for faith; be it blind or informed. If a religion can remain uncorrupted and pure, intent on good things, then it can do a lot of good, but in order to do that it must be built on a foundation that is solid, reasonable, logical, and full of a desire for truth, with enough humbleness to recognize its own flaws. Religions have flaws to be sure and many people have lost their connection to religion these days.

I hope to never see a day where humanity has lost its faith.

The Point Of Faith/Belief

A religious man, an agnostic and an atheist walked into a bar. They all sat at a table and had a round of drinks.

At one point in the evening during their conversations the religious man turns to the atheist and says "isn't God great?"

The atheist replied "I don't believe in God."

The two began to argue about the existence of God until at last the religious man said stubbornly "You cannot deny God!"

The atheist answered back "You cannot prove he exists!"

Fed up with the behavior of his friends, the agnostic broke into the conversation, putting himself between his two companions to stop the fighting. "Enough!" He said. "Both of you. You're both right, you can neither prove nor disprove God!" His outburst put a sour expression on his friend's faces so he turned to the religious man and told him "You need to calm down. Go order another round."

The religious man sighed and went to order more drinks.

While the religious man was busy the agnostic turned to the atheist "And you... I realize you don't believe in a higher power but what have you got to lose in considering that there may be more to the world than what you believe?"

The atheist was confused for a moment. It took him a while to realize he had simply been rude to the religious man's beliefs. He thought on in for a moment before he had an answer. "I suppose I don't have anything to lose." He replied. "Not even a soul from my standpoint."

The agnostic smiled and said "So, right or wrong, what's the harm in believing?"

This is just a silly anecdote but it speaks to an important point. We need to be tolerant of the beliefs of others or else we're just going to make each other volatile. It can be beneficial to consider the benefits granted by the views of others in order to strengthen our relationships and expand our own understanding.

With so much controversy as to the nature of existence, why should we believe in a higher power? Is it a search for truth or is it an exercise in mere superstition? In society today there are a lot of people with a menagerie of different opinions, some of which are mere ignorance and some of which strike a chord of truth. That said, intolerance is as strong as it ever was and the lively debate over whether or not there is a God is still present. So what is the point of having a faith?

The story above about three different kinds of beliefs illustrates an important point. It speaks to the intolerance of one viewpoint over another. In many religions it has been said that "disbelievers will abide in the fire", indicating that if you do not believe in a specific religion that your punishment at the end of your days will be Hell. Does the lack of faith really condemn? It is a puzzling question to be sure, so let's delve into the issue. First, we have to ask the right questions.

Is there a benefit to religious faith?
The simple answer: Yes.
People's belief in a higher power helps encourage them as they go through life to make good choices and perform good deeds. Those beliefs can help them to avoid selfish and destructive acts as well as to strive for a better world in which to live.

Sometimes those encouragements come in the form of incentives such as the notion of Heaven as a reward for a good life, or Hell as punishment for a bad one. In some religions the soul is obliterated completely at the end of a life for sinful behavior, and in others the bad parts are merely taken away and what is left over continues on to the next life. (Upanishads Vol 3 124)

If you ever want to find someone who is causing little harm and selflessly helping others, look no further than the dedicated faithful.

Is there a potential drawback to faithlessness?
The simple answer: Yes.

Our beliefs are core to our selves. You will never find something clung to more tightly than a belief. Zealously religious people will cling to their teachings even in the face of adversity up to and sometimes including their own demise. It is our nature to hold on to our beliefs. Without a strong belief we merely go through life acting and reacting based on our own desires or the influence of the world around us.

When a person considers how meaningful their life is on a grander scale, with a lack of divinity it seems we humans have no greater purpose. We simply are. So we live and die, suffer and enjoy and it doesn't matter. The problem with this perception is that sometimes suffering becomes unbearable and we ask ourselves why we should suffer at all since we're going to die anyway, and then suicidal thoughts are hastened and we leave this world prematurely. Faith helps us to endure that suffering because the power of our belief gives us a greater sense of purpose, whether it be God's divine plan or merely the idea of the oneness of everything.

Do we have to have faith in a higher power to do

good deeds and live a worthwhile life?

The simple answer: No.

But it sure helps.

It is not inconceivable that a person without any spiritual beliefs could make a tremendously good impact on the world. It is also not inconceivable that a person without spiritual beliefs could live a worthwhile life in the face of great suffering.

It isn't always the case, however. I've met a lot of selfish people who have spent their time concerned with their own happiness and wealth than with others, and typically those people have possessed a poor or underdeveloped faith or no faith at all.

Whether or not you believe in a higher power, the hope is that you give the possibility some thought. We have the potential to live a great and worthwhile life and, provided that the faith we might develop is built on a firm foundation and serves the greater good, we have nothing to lose by believing. God gave us eyes that we might see the truth and a discerning mind that we might realize it for what it is, nothing more and nothing less. God also gave us arms and legs that we might do something about it. Most importantly, God gave us the ability to endure through the hardships of our lives so that when we realize that the truth is not what we had believed, we can grow through it and become greater than we are.

God does not need our worship. We do. That's why faith is there: for us to grow, for us to understand, and for us to reach a greater state of being. Faith comes from all that surrounds us and God's good graces. I would hope that our faith should not come from the mouths of others, for man's words are subject to imperfections just as much as mankind is subject to imperfections. To take what is told to us as the foundation of our unwavering belief is to lead a blind faith. And like blindness, there is much stumbling and danger to be had when one cannot see. As such, we should discern for ourselves what is right, and have faith that God will help correct our mistakes to make us a better people. God gave us the freedom to choose of our own accord, not so that we could let others decide our faiths for us.

True Faith

To have faith means to possess a working belief about the truth of existence that, while it cannot be proven, it can be explored. To have faith means to act according to personal beliefs. To have faith means to strive for truth. If a faith is to be true and "protect and deliver us from evil", there are things that it must be and things it must not be.

A True Faith Is:

A true faith is tolerant of other faiths and religions. It does not force it's views on others. It does not convert, but is sought after.
A true faith is lived, not preached. It needs no church, for its temple is the believer. It needs no preacher for it continues through example, not rhetoric.
A true faith searches for the path of truth. A true faith is not accepted blindly, nor does it ignore the wisdom of reason.
A true faith is strong. It is incorruptible and steadfast in the face of adversity and gives us the courage to stand up for what is right. A true faith is not controlled by fear, nor does it make fearful.
A true faith is the ideal. It does not ally itself with factions, be they social, governmental, business or religious, but allies itself with ideals.
A true faith helps to create, not destroy. It does not kill. It spares non-believers and believers alike. It defends the just as well as the wicked and seeks the benefit of all.

A true faith does not spread hatred, but has an unending hope for goodness. It transforms our strongest loathing into the energy to resolve conflict.

A true faith is not petty. It is honorable, respectful, and kind. If it gives us the temperance to act appropriately, even in trying circumstances.

A true faith is patient, merciful, and understanding of mistakes. It gives us the power to forgive even our greatest enemies.

Above all, a true faith is worth having.

God

God vs. other worship

A simple truth: You can pray to whatever you want to. You can believe in whatever you wish. You have that ability and that right.

I have a hard time believing that a statue carved out of stone or forged in gold is going to do me a whole lot of good if I pray to it. I may as well be praying to a toaster. At least when I ask it of the toaster I may be given toast. The Old Testament in the bible contains a lot of stories about the tearing down of idols and false gods. There are especially a lot of stories about Baal and Ashera poles and sacrifices to otherworldly deities. The trouble is these practices were built more on superstition than upon actual truth. Sacrificing a bull to bring about the rain is fine and dandy, but unless there is an environmental change brought about by conditions that sacrificing a bull creates, the act is little more than superstition. A bull was sacrificed and it happened to rain, but when the bull was sacrificed and it didn't rain people felt it was their iniquity that prevented the powers that be from providing rain. (Stone Edition Chumash, The Haftaros Mattos 6, 5) Many years ago people didn't understand how the weather worked. This of course from a purely scientific view, but nonetheless an important part of the search for truth.

Another simple truth: Correlation does not imply causation. Just because one thing happens to trend in one direction while another thing trends in one direction does not mean that the one corresponds to the other. In an amusing observation it was determined that the average global temperature was increasing over the years. At the same time the number of pirates in the world had steadily decreased. Does this mean that the less pirates we have the warmer the world gets? Should we then increase the number of pirates to decrease the average global temperature? I highly suspect that such is not the case. Correlation does not imply causation. Sacrificing a bull does not bring the rain. These kinds of beliefs are the foundation of superstition. The foundation of truth is discovering why the average global temperature is rising, or why the number of pirates in the world has steadily decreased over the years, or why the rain falls or what real benefit there is to sacrificing a bull besides perhaps tasty beef stew.

We can believe whatever we wish but we should bare in mind that just because we believe something does not make it true. This goes for anything. It is possible that the beliefs I note here are not the truth. It is possible that the atheists are right and that there is no God. It is also possible that the atheists are wrong and there is a God. Or anywhere in between. Perhaps The Almighty Toast Lord is the greatest power in all creation! All I really wish to point out here is that belief and knowledge are two very different things and until something is concretely proved, speculation and belief are all we really have. It would be wise to pray to something that actually has the power to help, or else why pray at all? What really matters with belief is what good it does, both internally and externally. A faith that does not serve the world or serve the believer is probably not a faith worth having.

God Does Not Micromanage

You may have, in your travels, run across someone who was convinced that God was responsible for all of their problems. That God was purposefully smashing that person under His thumb at every turn as a form of cruelty for no other reason than to make that person suffer. Or perhaps God was punishing them tenfold for the few transgressions that person felt responsible for.

Perhaps you are one of those people.

If God is the single greatest force in existence, capable of all things, does it seem reasonable that such a powerful entity would spend its energy tweaking every second of every moment of a person's life just to cause them great suffering? Does it seem reasonable that part of "God's plan" is manipulating on the finest degree the life of any one person? If you know anything about business, you know very well that micromanagement breeds contempt and often very poor performance as a result. If God is so magnanimous and the most powerful entity in existence, then surely he is the greatest manager in existence. After all, he is managing all of creation. The best managers only tweak important things here and there and lets the business run itself. Do you really think that someone not getting a job or spilling a cup of coffee is so critical that the Universal Manager is responsible for making it happen? I have a hard time imagining that God is purposefully responsible for my stubbed toe.

Please consider that God does not micromanage. What reason does God have to do such a thing? That is not to discount a divine hand in the workings of the world, but to affirm the certainty of consequences for our own behavior. In short, God runs existence but we are responsible for the consequences of our actions. Typically, when we have problems, it is because we have set ourselves up for them. Spilling coffee happens because we are careless. Missed career paths happen because someone else is more qualified or the hiring agent is doing a poor job. My stubbed toe was my own fault, I admit. It is doubtful that these occurrences are the "will of God" but rather that they are the consequences of our actions and simply the natural flow of the way things are.

When you look at the possibilities of fate and the inter-connectivity of our lives as a species, as will be discussed later in Fate vs. Drive, it seems reasonable if not apparent that some things truly do have a divine hand guiding us in a specific direction but most things are a result of our own actions and desires.

Mankind desires, in the realm of spiritual belief, a God who is just and benevolent, who wants what is best for mankind. Instead of assuming that God is vicious and uncaring, why not spend our energy by putting our faith in a God worth believing in? After all, that is the point of faith, isn't it? I don't really care much to believe in The Great Tyrannical Bully. I don't feel that such belief is worth the effort.

To put it simply: We shouldn't blame all of our problems on God.

There is a position some people take that God is unchanging. When looking at God's role in our lives it is possible that god is not unchanging, but that God adapts and reacts. This allows for a God who plays an active part in everything. And at the same time, just because God adapts and reacts, does not mean that God changes, but is the same God. Just as we are the same human beings when we react. We may encounter differing circumstances, but we adapt to them to achieve our desired results. Maybe we can think of God like a river. Things in the river may over time alter the river's course, stop or increase its flow, and the river adapts to it. However, even as it adapts, it is still a river. It has not changed that state, just as God was, so God is.

As a testament to mankind's lack of understanding, we don't know what God has done or hasn't. Sometimes it is hard for us to accept that we made a mistake or to acknowledge the mistakes of others. We can say it's all Gods fault as much as we wish to remove blame from ourselves but we do not know it to be so. Just because we believe in something doesn't make it true. I do not recommend assigning blame when we have no cause to do so other than our own anger and selfish pride. Why would/should we worship God if God is cruel? We should have faith that God means well to us, that God is good and worthy of our praise, and that our misfortunes will be reconciled so long as we have faith. There is evidence all around us of good things, should we take the time to see them. Search high and far for them if you must. They are there. We can take comfort in that, and let if fuel our faith. There is always a potential for things to improve, even beyond the scope of our own limited imaginations. We may simply need faith to realize them.

In the Absence of God

As a musing supposition, consider this:
In the beginning there was nothing. Nothing is defined as the absence of everything. By the very definition of Nothing, there must needs be an Everything which Nothing is not. That Everything, which Nothing is not, could be referred to as God. After all, God is all.

If God created what we know as reality, what material did God use? So far as we've seen you can't make something out of nothing. If the only resources available were Nothing and Everything (God), then the only materials God had at God's disposal was God's self (Everything). Therefore, in this humble musing, God created reality out of God's self. Reality, made of God, by God, exists within nothing, but contains everything. Perhaps this is the nature of the universe.

If there was a way to return to a state where there was only Nothing, then Everything would need to be destroyed. Thus destruction is a component of God's absence. In that sense, evil could be considered the absence of God. However, if we were to return to a state of Nothing, we would be at the start once more, where in order to have that Nothing we must also have Everything which Nothing is not, and thus the Universe begins again. Perhaps this is the cycle of things.

The cyclical possibility described above implies that God cannot be destroyed because by definition God must exist, as we have defined God as Everything. If we start talking about science, there is only one thing that scientists currently believe cannot be destroyed, and that is energy. In that way, God is like energy. Everything has energy. In that respect, God could be everything.

The same cyclical definition notes that Nothing is required for existence, and in that respect, God is also nothing. Perhaps God is the void.

Confused yet?

Good.

This supposition seems in many ways silly. After all, it is perhaps simply a clever word play. A word play, no less, that mimics reality as perhaps one might see it. The point of this word play is to show how God is discussed by process of definition and how we tend to interpret God through metaphor. If we believe that God is all, it cannot be disproved by science because that is simply how we define God. If one were to define God as a golden statue (shame on you heathens!), science could not disprove that the statue was God because God had been defined as such. That is the nature of defining things. As Shakespeare said so famously in Romeo and Juliet, "a rose by any other name would smell as sweet". Of course, if the statue were God, it could be melted, fused into other materials or utterly destroyed by splitting the atoms that made it up like a nuclear bomb, but that is beside the point. It would be quite amusing to see mankind attempt to destroy Nothing in order to prevent Everything...

    Another way of saying almost the same things is this:
- All of this is. (whether illusory or real)
- Therefore it was conceived. (by my mind or by some other existence)
- That which conceived it is called God. (and it is no different than itself; the great creator, the way, Brahman, Allah, etc.)

    An interesting way of looking at the nature of existence comes from simple truth and logical inference. The Hindu faith looks at parts of existence like pieces of a pot. Each piece is still a part of the clay that is the pot. The pot and the clay are no different, nor are its pieces. (Upanishads Vol 2 235) It might look something like this:

    I am.
    We are.
    This is.
    I am a part of this.
    I am the same as this.
    I am this.
    I am.

    You may have run across (or be) someone who says "there is no God" and "show me the proof." Even the faithful beg and pray for God to send down some sign, some undeniable indication of divine presence to confirm that their beliefs are on the right track and that their suffering has a purpose. Even if that sign did come there would be many who would deny its divine origin. They would ascribe its source to an alien life form, strange energy or some other scientific explanation, or a ghost, spiritual entity or "magic". To stubborn skeptics it would not matter the origin, they are bound to call it anything but God. That is what it means to have a hardened heart. You can call God by another name be it science or alien or whatever you will, but calling it another name does not change what it is.

"Atman [God] cannot be proved by mere argumentation. No finality about a supramental entity can be reached by mere argumentation. A disputant's opinion based on reasoning reflects only the state of his mind. Atman transcends all mental states."(The Upanishads Vol I, 134)

As contended by the faithful: God is all. The universe is, and it was made to be. God is the source of all creation. There is nothing that is that wasn't created by God. You can call it the big bang or cyclical universe but at it's source is God. And God is all things. There is no thing that isn't a part of everything, and God is all. In other words, God is defined as the source of creation. We look around us and see all the proof we need. We are here, and the world is here and it is wondrous and awesome. You can call all creation something else if you wish, but we speak of the same thing albeit by a different name. Calling a rock a sheep won't change the rock from what it is. Calling the source of all creation El, Hashem, God or the devil won't change it from what it is.

"And if ye shall say there is no law, ye shall also say there is no sin. If ye shall say there is no sin, ye shall also say there is no righteousness. And if there be no righteousness there be no happiness. And if there be no righteousness nor happiness there be no punishment nor misery. And if these things are not there is no God. And if there is no God we are not, neither the earth; for there could have been no creation of things, neither to act nor to be acted upon; wherefore, all things must have vanished away."(Smith 430)

If we're going to start somewhere in the argument for or against the source of all creation, let's look at some of the established concepts that are commonly believed, and why they don't seem to add up within the context of existential belief.
An inherent problem with the traditionally presented Great Creator of All Things comes from the following assumptions:

First: God created everything
Second: God is all powerful
Third: God is all knowing
Fourth: God is benevolent

The first inherent problem is this: If god created everything (and I mean EVERYTHING) and there is such a thing within everything as evil, then God created evil. Additionally, if God is all knowing then God created evil knowing the consequences thereof and the damage it would wreak upon his creations. In essence, God created "the devil". Next, if we understand absolute benevolence as only acting for good and never acting for bad then what follows is a contradiction of points. Therefore, if God is benevolent then God would not have knowingly created evil. If that is true, then God could not have created everything, or else God did not know the consequences of his creation.
As you can see, by applying logic to the four assumptions, we encounter impossibilities. The only way to make sense of the traditional assumptions is either to modify or deny one of them. Of course, the easiest is to deny the complete benevolence of God. Many believe that

God is neither good nor evil but is always just. To completely deny a benevolent nature and declare instead that God is one hundred percent malevolent, would result in the same contradiction, because then God could not have knowingly created good.

So, we must find a middle ground by applying a modification. The worst is that God is malevolent but not completely, and thus we have a cruel God with no end to our suffering (enter The Great Tyrannical Bully). The better option, in my opinion, is to acknowledge a God who is mostly benevolent, but has allowed humanity the capacity to make itself suffer, in order for humanity to desire the good that is possible through its actions and development. The reason I find this a better option is quite simple: I have no desire to worship a cruel God, and a God worth believing in is a benevolent one.

The second modification to these four assumptions is that God did not create everything. This would deny our definition of God as the source of all creation. Since God is defined as the source of all creation, then we wouldn't be able to continue this line of thinking since we would be confusing definitions at that point.

The third modification is that God doesn't know everything. It is possible that God made the universe not because God knew what the result would be, but because God wanted to see what would happen. I could not say with certainty that I believe this to be true, but the notion of it's possibility is certainly one to spark conversation. When we think about a God that doesn't know but wants to know, we start down the path to understanding the reason for all existence. I for one feel we are just a tad too small to comprehend such a colossal reason, but who knows. Perhaps with meditation and some elbow grease we might divine something from such a notion.

The fourth modification is that God is not all powerful. The way I like to view this notion is this: God is

not all powerful but God is the most powerful. This is the
idea that there are things that God is not capable of, such as
destroying itself and all creation, or perhaps the amount of
influence it has over its "body". Think for a moment about
your kidney. It is certainly a part of your body, and
functions within you, but you cannot tell it to wither and
die with your mind. You cannot transform your kidney into
a heart or a lung, or tell it to become a toaster no matter
how badly you want toast. It functions as a part of you yet
you cannot exercise your will over it. If we view existence
as the body of God, as compared to our own bodies,
without tools or anything outside of itself, perhaps God
only has power over some parts, and other parts function
involuntarily. A strange notion, to be sure, but interesting to
think about. I personally do not feel that this is the truth,
but as someone who seeks truth without possessing
compete understanding of all things, I can acknowledge the
possibility that I am wrong.

    These four modifications of our assumptions of God
may not be the truth, or they may approach it. It is difficult
to be certain. Perhaps some of them are on the right track.
Perhaps it is a combination of them that approaches the
truth. Who could say? The reason I point them out is to
suggest to those who do not believe in a higher power
because they see logical fallacies within the original four
assumptions that these beliefs are just that: assumptions.
When you modify those assumptions, God becomes a
logical possibility once more.

    I have heard many times that logic and religion are
not compatible. I do not believe that even for an instant.
The existence I am familiar with follows logical reasoning.
To me, God created a logical existence, so why should faith
be incompatible with it since faith is a part of the logical
world? If existence follows logic and reasoning, why
should faith depart from it? I've said before that Faith,
Philosophy and Science all seek the same truth. They are

not incompatible, but interconnected. If you want to see that in action, look to moments in history where science, religion or philosophy have made great leaps. You will see that when one evolves, so too do the others. That is the power of the search for truth.

If we seek to improve and redefine our faith humanity will move forward in its understanding and development as a culture and species. Through our reinvention we can achieve a greater good, and through it a better us if we are charitable to the notion of a benevolent God. Additionally, If you do not believe in God, I encourage you to keep your eyes and mind open, because if you assume that atheism is the certain absolute truth, you will be just as blind as any overzealous Christian, Muslim or Buddhist, etc.

Bigotry

The Blind Men and the Elephant

There is a parable about blind men and an elephant. It has been retold in innumerable ways by innumerable people, but the message still remains the same. The story goes something like this:

There were five men who were blindfolded and brought into a room with an elephant. They were asked to describe the elephant without being told what it was. They each touched a different part of the elephant and then afterward began to tell each other what they had experienced.

The first man said "it is like a piece of heavy cloth" because he had touched the elephant's ear.

"No it isn't." The second man protested. "It is like a great python," for he had touched the elephant's trunk.

"You're both wrong." Said the third. "It is like a rope," for he had grabbed only the tail.

The fourth one shook his head confused. "What are you talking about? It is like a wall." For he had touched only the elephant's side.

"You're all wrong. It is nothing like any of that," said the fifth. "It is clearly like the trunk of a tree," for he had touched the elephant's leg.

The men argued and argued with each other about what the elephant was. Finally, their blindfolds were removed and they could see that none of them had been correct, and that they had each only sampled a portion of the elephant.

Religions throughout the world might be compared to the blind men in this story. Every religion has its own thoughts and beliefs about the true nature of existence, but religions often scorn the beliefs of other religions. In truth there is a good chance that none of them are completely right, but most of them have at least discovered a partial truth.

There are several different religions that are dominant in the world today. Islam, Christianity, Catholicism, Judaism, Mormonism, Taoism, Hinduism and Buddhism, just to name a few. If we try to understand each one, what we discover is that there is wisdom in all of them. We might also discover that there are things in each of them that do not hold true. Each person may find different things they agree with and disagree with, but there is a good chance that the truth lies not in one dogma or another, but in the culmination of our search for truth present in all of them. That is the search for a true faith.

The search for truth by means of the development of faith is exactly like the men trying to discover what they were touching in the room with the elephant. The search of truth is not like the men telling each other that they are wrong about their assessment of the elephant. When we search for truth by developing faith, we cannot consider just our own views but the views of others. That isn't to say that we should believe everything we are told, but merely that we consider what others tell us and contemplate how that may or may not fit into the truth of this world. That is the nature of being open minded.

It seems impossible for a person to experience and know everything about everything in existence. I think if I should try that my very head might explode. Many would argue that to do so would be to become God-like. By definition, to know everything is to be omniscient. Our minds are quite small in the grand scheme of things (roughly the size of two fists put together) and in many instances we have to depend on the word of others just to function in the world we live in. While we should be careful of what we choose to believe, it isn't damning to consider the views of others. Merely informative. If the blindfolded men in the story had left the room and collaborated over what they had seen, perhaps drawing it on a piece of paper, it is possible that they may have drawn something that resembled an elephant. Perhaps not. It wasn't clear if the blind men were good artists. Regardless, the men would most likely be closer to the truth if they considered the possibility that each of them had found a partial truth than they were by assuming that all of the others were wrong and only their own experiences were the truth.

The Priest and the Preacher

As mentioned before, a true faith is not preached, it is lived. It needs no preacher for it continues through example, not rhetoric. This may seem somewhat confusing, so please allow me to clarify. First, we should look at the definitions of two seemingly similar, yet very different things: Priests and preachers.

A priest is defined as a person whose office it is to perform religious rites or make sacrificial offerings. Such a person is ordained to the sacerdotal or pastoral office or might be known as a member of the clergy or simply a minister. (Dictionary.com Priest) In shorter and easier to understand words, they are put into position by the church they are a part of.

A priest is a position in a hierarchy, even if a very small one in the instance of rural churches. That means that they are part of religion as explained above. Most people within a religion look to a priest as someone with wisdom from whom they might seek guidance.

It should be noted that nowhere within the definition of a priest is there a necessity for preaching.

A preacher is a person whose occupation or function is to preach gospel, proclaim or make things known by sermon, advocate or inculcate religious or moral truth in speech or writing, and to give earnest advice (usually on religious or moral subjects). The word preach is also associated with performing the above in an obtrusive or tedious way. (Dictionary.com, Preacher, Preach) Words can be preached on the street, in a church, at work, etc. While there is often little credibility given to a preacher by people who do not know the person preaching, there are occasionally people who stop and listen to whatever message is being preached. That being said, who is to say if a preacher is a moral person, wise or intelligent when so little is known about that person? This is why a discerning mind is necessary to recognize truth, and why a faith must be taught through action rather than words.

    Anyone can see the harm a bigoted person causes by the suffering left in their wake. Bigots spread hatred and estrangement, causing rifts in society. However, when it is only bigoted words that are present and not actions, that suffering may not be directly observable which is why it is so difficult to fight against bigotry.

    People are often prideful about their own actions, insisting that they have done no wrong. That makes it more difficult to see the damage caused by our own actions. If the words of someone seem good but the actions of that person are hateful and discriminatory, and we act upon those words, we open ourselves up to the same hateful and discriminatory behavior. Often we do not recognize our own mistakes until it is too late.

    A preacher is not necessarily a priest, and vise versa. A preacher can be anyone, whether appointed or not, wise or foolish, goodly or wicked, spiritual or faithless, and thus is defined only by their decision to preach. By this very definition, there is a great deal of potential to preach misconceptions, fears and irrational messages, much to the detriment of anyone who might listen. When people believe blindly what a preacher says, as in a blind faith, it can lead undue hatred, religious wars, intolerance, estrangement and poor choices of behavior.

Preaching is obtrusive. Even if the message of the preacher is not heard, often the act of preaching itself causes irritability in those nearby. Nobody likes to have someone else's views forced upon them. Humans like to decide things for themselves. Therefore it is best to keep one's faith to the self instead of preaching it to others.

At the University I attended, every year, without fail during the spring season on a particularly nice day, there was a man would make his way to the center of campus to a very high traffic area and begin to spout all sorts of religious rhetoric. He would posture and shout and make powerful accusations about the sins of the students and proclaim that he knew the will of God and that we all would burn in Hell unless we atoned for our transgressions. The first year I witnessed this man preaching was my freshman year, and he revisited every year until I graduated, still spouting the same message. As far as I know he may still be doing the same thing.

What this man was doing is known as preaching. In this instance, he was preaching to people who had no idea who he was and probably thought he was crazy. He might very well have been. He did not know the people he was shouting at, nor did they know him. He did not know which students were transgressors and which were truly innocent. He preached as if they were all wicked and deserving of the fires of Hell. He had a message he wanted to convey concerning the spiritual and moral nature of the world.

The effect of this man's behavior was this: As students walked by they pointed, laughed, made derogatory comments and continued walking by. Most of them turned their ears off the moment they recognized the message he was trying to deliver. A lot of the students walked away a little angry or at the very least in less of a good mood than when they had left their dorm rooms. Occasionally, some brave individual would decide that this man was out of line and approach him in order to talk some sense into the man. Oh boy... If I thought the preaching man was angry at the world before, it was nothing compared to his reaction then. No matter what reasonable thing the confronter said, no matter how much he tried to agree with this man, even, the preacher would not even bother to listen. He would instead shout more or quote scripture tailored specifically to suit his agenda, never mind whether or not he was saying the same thing the student was saying. In the end, the confronter left angry and the preacher continued to preach. I imagine a good many students were turned off from religion at least a little by the actions of this man, and certainly none of them were leaping to go join this man at his own local church assembly.

Did anyone really listen to his message and take it to heart? Probably not. If they had for some reason I imagine the result would have been another person blindly assuming that everyone was evil and that they were all going to burn unless they conformed to the scriptures, performing the same act as the preacher and spreading messages of intolerance and fire and brimstone.

Does that sound like a positive message of peace?

A priest is by definition a part of a religious system. The potential for such an individual to mislead their followers is great. In such hierarchical systems, if there is a flaw in an individual of great influence, it often spreads fear, ignorance or misconceptions as well as irrationality to those who follow the flawed individual. When a priest is irrational about tolerance or views of right or wrong, their actions (be it verbal or otherwise) are observed by the members of the congregation. When people look to a priest for wisdom and guidance, they are not always able to discern good advice from bad, and thus whatever poor beliefs are held by the priest can spread to the congregation. This is why priesthood can be very dangerous.

As proven through the test of time, hierarchies become dangerous over time as the imperfections of those at the top seep down to those who follow them. Priesthood is misleading. Even Peter acknowledged that all of us are priests in our own way (International Bible, 1 PET, 2:5), and through that philosophy the hierarchy of modern religion disappears. When all of us are priests, nobody is treated as having more or less authority on a subject, and therefore we can lead ourselves instead of being misled by others. That makes us accountable for our own actions. Nobody wants to be misled. Many of us want to have a form of guidance. Therefore it is good to acknowledge everyone as equals and seek truth instead of submitting to the opinions of others.

Let us take a moment to look at the European crusades. During the crusades great wars were fought against people of differing religions. Didn't the church of Christ abhor killing and violence? So how did it come to pass that such wars ravaged Europe and the Middle East between the 11th and 15th centuries? Were they really living true to their faiths? One could easily argue no. They were listening to the religious powers at the time, fighting for territory and political power. What did the soldiers do as they moved through enemy lands? They pillaged. They took whatever they wanted and whatever they found valuable. It is doubtful that the leaders of those churches who went to war were pure and righteous. In this case the flaws of those in power trickled down to their followers and the result was death spread throughout the land. If the heads of the churches hadn't condoned the crusades the crusades would not have happened. That is the trouble with corruption within a hierarchy. As the saying goes: "The fish rots from the head".

Priests and preaching can have a negative influence over society, whether we want to admit it or not. That said, not all priests are bad and certainly not everything preached carries a bad message. However, we humans are imperfect. So too are our words. If we are going to cultivate a true and lasting faith, perhaps we should avoid hierarchy and preaching in order to mitigate their potential to mislead and corrupt.

The Bigot

"Accept him whose faith is weak, without passing judgment on disputable matters. One man's faith allows him to eat everything, but another man, whose faith is weak, eats only vegetables. The man who eats everything must not look down on him who does not, and the man who does not eat everything must not condemn the man who does, for God has accepted him. Who are you to judge someone else's servant? To his own master he stands or falls. And he will stand, for the Lord is able to make him stand.

One man considers one day more sacred than another; another man considers every day alike. Each one should be fully convinced in his own mind. He who regards one day as special, does so to the Lord. He who eats meat, eats to the Lord, for he gives thanks to God; and he who abstains does so to the Lord and gives thanks to God." (International Bible, Romans. 14:6 1-6)

Bigotry is defined as the stubborn and complete intolerance of any creed, belief, or opinion that differs from one's own. A bigot is defined as a person who is completely intolerant of any other creed, belief or opinion. (Dictionary.com Bigot, Bigotry)

Let's take a moment to understand bigotry more in depth. The important determining factor in bigotry is complete intolerance. Intolerance should not be confused with differing opinion or disbelief, but rather a refusal to respect beliefs or behaviors other than one's own. To be tolerant of someone's beliefs is not necessarily to believe in them, but rather to acknowledge that the opinion should be respected. This is more a social notion of how to properly behave toward your fellow human than it is a question of who is right and who is wrong. Being disrespectful of a differing belief can range anywhere from insulting someone to acting out against them with violence and aggression. In many instances, bigotry takes the form of trying to force one's beliefs on another person.

    If you want to you can think of this book as a way to impress upon others an opinion. However, the expression of an opinion and the act of bigotry are very different. The difference in bigotry and the sharing of opinions openly is expressed very well by the function of literature. When a book is presented to you, typically, nobody is forcing you to read it. Nobody is holding your head down in front of the pages demanding you to recite it back, nor are you required to accept and believe in its contents. If they are, I would strongly encourage you to run. Your own opinion might be called in to question by the contents of the writing, and certainly if you were reading a work of bigotry your opinions or beliefs might be insulted. However, you can always put the book down. (In fact, I the author would encourage you to do so if this book offends. The purpose of this writing is not to insult any religion or belief, but rather to encourage an open mind and to discourage bigotry, which is why it is written down instead of being preached on a street corner.) A bigot would not let you put the book down. A bigot wants you to conform to their own belief because they value their own opinions and beliefs more than yours and do not possess the compassion and courage necessary to allow for free thought.

"Not knowing is true knowledge
Presuming to know is a disease.
First realize that you are sick;
Then you can move toward health."
> (Tao Te Ching 71)

     In order to better guard ourselves against bigotry we must first understand its cause. By understanding its cause we can start to identify how to encourage ourselves and others to avoid it.

     So, why do we have bigots? What causes people to act in such intolerant ways? Typically, bigotry is caused by three factors. The first of these factors is ignorance. Remember how we talked about how firmly people cling to their beliefs? When a person spends twenty-five years being fed the same rhetoric, they tend to believe it completely and perhaps blindly. They may not be able to wrap their minds around anything else. They wouldn't know how to. People have a tendency to avoid things they do not understand and so they forget that people with differing beliefs are part of the same human race and are trying to embrace truth just as much as the ignorant are. Ignorant bigotry causes estrangement and separation between people. When we fear the beliefs and opinions of others we are more likely to avoid the company of others.

     The second of these factors is pride. Pride is an expression of selfishness concerning one's importance which will be talked about later in this book. When people are prideful of their beliefs, they view themselves above others of differing beliefs. A prideful bigot places themselves higher than others, forgets the humanity of others and treats others as infantile or less than human. Prideful bigotry quickly leads to disrespect and resentment between the bigot and others. Resentment leads to violence and aggression. When we see ourselves as high others become low.

The third of these factors is fear. People are often afraid of things they do not understand. When we are afraid of something we enter a "fight or flight" response. Running away from differing beliefs leads to ignorance and estrangement. Fighting against differing opinions often leads to violence and the violation of basic human rights. When we fear others we forget that they are human just like us. The fearful bigot lashes out and harms others out of reflex and runs and hides, increasing their own intolerance and ignorance. The only way to eliminate fearful bigotry is to educate and encourage people to obtain the skills necessary to search for truth. If people don't know how to search for truth, they become susceptible to misconceptions or else they learn nothing and do not search for truth at all. This leads to ignorance.

Bigotry is a disrespectful act that encourages ignorance, disrespect and creates barriers and chasms between the people of this earth. Bigotry makes people angry. It persecutes and discriminates. It is the result of ignorance, pride and fear, all of which can lead to selfish, intentional and destructive acts.

There is a flower shop in the town where I grew up that had been in business for many years. The bulk of their business was weddings and other social occasions, while of course catering to people who simply wished to purchase a bouquet for a friend or loved one. This flower shop, just like other businesses, was open to the public as is the nature of capitalism. They did business with everyone equally. Or at least they should have. At one point several years ago the flower shop was asked to provide flowers for a wedding. Nothing unusual there. However, the individuals who were getting married to each other were both men. The flower shop refused to provide them with service since the soon to be married were homosexual. Now, I won't speak as to the morality or immorality of homosexuality. I'll let humanity figure that one out. The flower shop was expressing their own bigotry against homosexual marriage by acting intolerant. While a business has a right to serve whom it will, we should be treating others respectfully regardless of whether or not their beliefs and behaviors vary from our own. It is more than likely that the flower shop had sold their wares to people who committed sinful behaviors of one kind or another. There is little doubt of that. It is not like the flower shop knew all of the details of every one of their customers. If the flower shop considered homosexuality to be sinful, what then is the difference between selling their wares to say thieves and homosexual men? It is the refusal to respect others. The flower shop expressed a complete intolerance not typical of their day to day business due to something that differed from their beliefs.

So, right or wrong, what was the result? The couple was angry, to be sure. The event was reported in the news, inflaming an already heated argument around the topic of gay marriage and other such issues. It encouraged volatile behavior and spurned on discussions between differing viewpoints that may have led to torn relationships and hatred. It increased the estrangement between people in the town. Again, I cannot say that gay marriage is right or wrong since I'm not God and I don't get to make that determination, but I can say that the behavior of the flower shop was an intentional, selfish and destructive act that caused harm to the community. It was bigotry.

This is just one example of the kind of things that happen in the world. If we are to grow together as a people so that we can survive whatever hardships are coming down the road, then we must develop a culture where there is less bigotry. Otherwise, when it matters most, we will be too busy fighting against each other to work together for the greater good. That path will lead to mankind's destruction, not its betterment.

"Failing to realize that his idea of Reality, being only a product of the imagination, is in no way different from other ideas, he becomes intolerant. This is a mistake generally committed by fanatics, who do not see that their views have no more validity than those of others." (The Upanishads 269)

Bigotry is not the expression of an opinion but rather the act of complete intolerance and disrespect to views other than one's own. Bigotry causes hatred and estrangement and encourages ignorance. We can have our own views without being completely intolerant and disrespectful of other views. To do so we must learn to be humble, courageous and informed.

Ouroboros

      Ouroboros is a symbol that goes back at least as far as 14th century B.C.. The symbol is a snake circling around and devouring its own tail. It represents the cyclical nature of things as well as rebirth, much like that of the phoenix. It can also represent a power or force that can never be extinguished. In addition to continual renewal it also represents continual destruction within a cycle.
      The ideas behind this symbol are subtle but nonetheless important to religious education. Humanity has followed the same cyclical nature for thousands of years. We grow, we create, we argue, we war, we struggle, we find peace, we grow, we create, etc. To acknowledge the cyclical nature of man is to understand what prevents

humanity from creating lasting peace, utopia, and truly serving the greater good.

To break things down into a simplified version: First, man seeks selfish gain, then man subjugates man. Man seeks freedom from his oppressors and so flees to a place where freedom can reign. Once free, man seeks selfish gain. Then man subjugates man, and seeks freedom; and so the cycle continues.

When left to our own devices as a society we tend to cause harm to ourselves, and then we run from our own wrongdoing. But what happens when there is nowhere left to run? As a species we have already reached the western most continent and spread across the world. Eventually we may flee to other planets, but for the time being we are running out of places to flee. If the self-eating snake were to devour itself faster than it could grow, eventually it would consume itself. The cycle would continue but when the body could no longer grow fast enough to escape the jaws of the snake it would at last devour itself entirely. The result is a shrinking cycle. The circle of Ouroboros would shrink until the head ate itself up, so to speak. Destruction would reign until there is enough room for the cycle to start again anew. With the invention of nuclear weaponry it is possible that humankind could completely extinguish itself in the blink of an eye. In that sense we may have reached a time where the cycle ends by devouring itself completely.

Or...

As an alternative to mankind's continual destructive nature, Ouroboros could cease devouring itself and allow itself to grow and flourish. Ouroboros also represents the force of something that cannot be extinguished. Mankind has overcome many obstacles in its history and will continue to persevere in the future.

These are two ways to look at the concept of Ouroboros if it were to change due to circumstances being what they have never been before. We are rapidly filling up the world with people. It is possible that we could create a world free from our own evil, though one could easily argue that such ends would be nearly impossible to reach. If escaping evil were the desired outcome we would have to obtain it through action and dedication and much of that action would be driven by faith. If we are going to accomplish the end of a destructive cycle, perhaps a world with the most good and the least evil, what better time than when we have run out of places to flee? The process that is required to break the cycle is certainly difficult but ultimately simple: Mankind has developed many great things in its time through science and philosophy. One thing we have yet to accomplish is a lasting culture of tolerance and compassion. If we can grow as a society and learn to become more selfless as a whole, the selfish desire to consume lessens and we cease to follow the same cycle we've followed for thousands of years. That is the freedom humanity so desperately seeks: Freedom from abuse and oppression. The only thing standing in our way is ourselves. It is despairing to see humanity fall victim to the same bad habits over and over again.

"A well-developed culture requires wisdom, power, wealth and service. Wisdom is the foundation, power is its protector, wealth helps in its dissemination, and service keeps the whole social order going. This is the basis of the caste system in India. The four castes discharge their four appointed functions. These distinctions are found also among the gods. The four castes – like the head, arms, thighs, and feet of a man – are interdependent. The welfare of one means the welfare of all. There is no question of the exploiting of one by another."
    (Upanishads Vol 3 127)

    One could argue that the end of the Ouroboros cycle is something that many religions seek but have failed to obtain. Through the development of a faith worth having, however, perhaps it could be realized. And it starts with the end of intolerance. If intolerance is eliminated from our culture, beliefs and opinions are allowed to develop and grow and we would be free to express, consider and rethink those opinions and beliefs as a culture rather than a bunch of squabbling individuals.

One person can process and cultivate a single belief from a single viewpoint. However, Truth is often not visible from a single viewpoint but from many. Billions of people cultivating a belief are more likely to discover truth than a single individual because the truth would be seen from billions of angles. This processing power can only be utilized if beliefs and opinions are respected and considered even if they are ill founded or wrong. Discovering the truth is not just about recognizing things that are true but also recognizing things that are not true. If a faith truly worth having was developed as a global culture it is possible we could start to act selflessly as a whole.

Ouroboros represents the cycle of mankind. In being open to possibilities, it's symbolism is not necessarily permanent as we continue to grow and adapt as a species. Without understanding and effort, however, we are sure to continue with the same habits we've exhibited for millennia.

43

Foundational Principles

The Path

Many religious philosophies regard life as a path we walk down. As the metaphor goes, when we are righteous we are on the path. When we stray we are off the path. For example, Mormonism's The Book of Mormon says there is a narrow path to walk to obtain righteousness. (Book of Mormon, 2 NEPHI, 31:9) The Tao translates literally as "The Way", regarding life and existence as some sort of path as well. If we think of life as a journey through available choices and time itself, rather than a singular pathway through a forest that is narrow and strictly defined, we allow for gray areas and can open our minds to truth.

With all the gray areas in life and obstacles that get in the way it seems more likely that the way to righteousness is like finding your way through a swamp; multiple paths, dead ends, walking through mire, nothing to guide you but what you can see in front of you. Swamps are difficult to navigate and often a person might not only lose their way but find themselves unable to see the way through the swamp. Sometimes we make the wrong choice and the result is making a misstep into swamp water. Sometimes we get lost and lose the path completely, and it seems like the only way to return to the direction we want to go is by wading through swamp until we can find a patch of land to stand on to get our bearings. In this sense, there is not a narrowly defined pathway, but no path at all. Merely a stretch of swamp with sections of land and water that stretch out between where we are and where we should go to achieve that righteous state. Taoism would say that in going with the flow of life, we try to reach the other side by following the bits of land before us. Sometimes when an obstacle blocks the way we must step aside and go around, but if we do this we muddy our feet in the process. If we climb the obstacle, it is a struggle and certainly harder than going around, but at least we keep ourselves clean. That is why it is good to not be lazy. It has been said that in order to obtain heaven we must keep our gaze fixed on God. In the metaphor of the swamp I would present "keeping our gaze fixed on God" as keeping our bearings as to which direction leads us from the swamp, much like a compass.

Our choices in life are not always clear or simple. A narrow but defined path doesn't always hold true to the circumstances of our life. Sometimes we have nothing but bad choices available because of the decisions we've made and it is hard to return to a place where good decisions are clear and available.

So, what is the point of walking this path? Many of us ask this question. The answer is sometimes difficult to see. Some of us even tire of searching for it. But we continue to seek an answer to this question because it is worthy of our pursuit. Many believe that there is one true nature to existence. Not three or seven or any other seemingly important number. The universe is one way. Truth is not subjective but objective, as some may tell you. Science believes it, as does some philosophy. Religious beliefs (though each religion seems to disagree with the others) think along the same lines as well. If our existence is one way, one truth, then what we seek is a means to express it in a faith that seeks it, lives it, and adds to it, not one that obscures and takes away from it. We desire a true faith. One that adheres to good and righteousness, and doesn't push humanity toward its own demise. "It deprives not of reason, nor are they exhausted therewith." (The Holy Qu'ran, Ch. 37, 47)

By definition, the act of understanding implies there is something to understand that is not understood and is a mystery. If we are to understand, we must begin at a place without understanding and from there discover the great mystery. It is not a path that we can always see ahead of us as in the swamp. There isn't a magical answer to "how do I discover the meaning of life?" Furthermore, it cannot be sought with expectations, or else the truth will not be found. If we seek truth with our own expectations, what we discover is modified by what we hope to discover, instead of truth. Therefore we cannot be blind to the truth, nor can we seek a faith that suits our own selfish desires. It would be like trying to navigate through a swamp by saying "first I will go left, then I will go straight and then I will turn right. I won't encounter any obstacles and I will always be able to see the path clearly" before ever having entered the swamp. Just as we do not get to decide how the swamp is laid out, we should not seek truth with expectations.

  We might ask ourselves what is a true faith? What qualities does it possess that are worth striving for?

  There is a faith worth believing in, and I hope that we may find it. My hope is that in reading this, you will ask these questions and hopefully many more.

  Let's spend a moment talking about intelligence. After all, it is one of humanity's greatest gifts. There are various levels of intellect throughout humanity. Some people we call smart or wise. Others we rudely call stupid or foolish. However, even those who do not learn quickly are still capable of learning. It may take more time and more effort. Much as it would take someone severely out of shape with a terrible metabolism to become a star athlete. It takes time, but it is possible. The best part is, even the weakest or most uncreative person is capable of developing a rich and fulfilling faith. It takes no talent, or gift, or noble birth. It merely requires three things: time, effort, and patience. Too many people leave their faith alone and untended and expect it to serve them well, but that faith becomes like a garden. If you leave it to its own devices it will wither and die or grow wild and rampant, filled with weeds and rot. However, if you nourish it and seek to develop it, it will flourish and grow into something both beautiful and fruitful. Standing still at a place in the swamp will not help us reach the end. We have to walk the path, not just stand on it.

One of the problems with faith arises when we want a simple answer to a big question. Perhaps our lives are so busy we don't seem to think we have the time to find the answer. We want a quick fix. Unfortunately, there is no simple answer to those big questions. In faith, when a simple answer is given, it often leads to misconceptions, ignorance, and a weak faith. Faith has depth. Easy answers give us an incomplete vision of truth, which does not serve us well.

Faith is not something that is brought to us like a bag of groceries or that falls into our laps like fruit off a tree. It is a path we must continue to walk down. It is something we create and develop throughout our lives. Many times we stop moving down the path, have to backtrack, and sometimes we leave it altogether. At times, it is difficult to walk that path. We deal with struggles every day. Our lives are filled with loss, pain, regret, sorrow and turmoil. That's a part of what it means to live. Sometimes we even think we're walking that path but we're just regurgitating the same religious rhetoric we've been fed since we were young and are walking around in circles, moving no closer to our goal. Sometimes we forget the path altogether and do great wrongs by those around us. It is during those times, and those moments in our life that are filled with great turmoil, that we should return to developing our faith. When we are confronted with obstacles on the path we must overcome them instead of taking the easy route by stepping in the mire. Overcoming obstacles is what makes us strong. That struggle brings us closer to truth than a lifetime of repetition and blind following. If we remember to keep traveling the path and continue onward, even if only slowly, the result is a stronger faith.

The purpose of this book is to arm you with greater understanding and encourage the open mind necessary to fight against religious bigotry. In order to accomplish this, we must understand the building blocks of morality and religion in order to stamp out that blind ignorance and intolerance expressed in bigoted people. Thus, we must look at the truth of the world we live in; things we consider to be good, things we consider evil and other things inherent in religion. Furthermore, we must understand why those things hold true in order to gain understanding. Next we will look at the foundational principles of moral and immoral action and other truths more closely.

Simple Truths

To even talk about faith we have to consider that which we know to be true. After all, faith should be based on truth, not superstition, shouldn't it? The world can be a very complicated and misleading place. Which of us is to say what is an illusion, what is not, and what is simply not understood? There are many opinions as to what is true and why it is true.

When trying to understand something it is easier to look at 'what' than to look at 'why'. That is the power of observation. Often, 'why' is based on an incomplete perception. So, to start our search for truth, we must begin with 'what'. Until we have great wisdom and understanding, we should start with the simplest of things so as to strengthen our current understanding. We should begin with simple truths.

Throughout this work I will point out simple truths

as they become relevant. You may find that my interpretation of those truths does not agree with you and that is fine. The hope is merely that they help you think and help you reach your own conclusions.

There are some important, simple truths that have a great deal to do with what makes us human and are very relevant to the search for a true faith. Firstly, we have emotions. We experience hate and fear, love and joy, jealousy and pride. Part of being human is the emotions we feel. Secondly, we have senses. We have sight and hearing, we taste, we touch, we smell. We feel pain and pleasure, we see the world around us, and we interact with it. Part of being human is our perceptions of the world.

As to why we have emotions and why we have senses, who could say? To guess at that would be to guess the purpose of our very existence. No doubt the answer is quite complex and profound. However, what we can seek to understand is the benefit of those emotions and the benefit of our senses if we take a moment to consider them.

Let's start with something provocative, just to get the brain juices flowing: Hate.

It is difficult to see the benefit of hate. In this day and age hate has become a nasty word that many of us wish to do away with. So, why do we hate? It is part of what we are; one of those emotions mentioned earlier. At first glance it seems that hate only causes misery and suffering among our kind. So why were we given such a thing? Why would a benevolent God give us the capacity to hate? How could such a negative emotion have a positive impact in our lives? Or is it merely an obstacle to be overcome?

In definition, hatred means to dislike intensely or passionately, or to have a severe aversion to someone or something. When we hate other people, or hate our selves and the world we live in, the result is typically damaging. Hatred fuels murders, crime, abuse and many other poor forms of behavior.

However, when we hate things like selfishness, bigotry, meaningless violence and other negative things, the result is a drive for change, which helps us grow. As a species, when we hate something we have a choice. We can either try to live without that thing or learn to tolerate it, which is a sign of strength. Humanity at the end of World War II hated the endless bloodshed and the atrocities visited during the war. That hatred gave birth to compassion, tolerance, peace and prosperity. That is perhaps an oversimplification of the times, but it is nonetheless true. Perhaps viewing hatred as something that is not purely negative might lead us to understand more about ourselves and the world than simply viewing it as an absolute wrong.

The simple truth: We experience hatred.

It seems likely that we have hate for a reason whether it is an obstacle or a boon. It is when we allow hate to control our actions that hate becomes a catalyst for evil. Rather, we should use it as a driving force for goodly action. In controlling our hate, we utilize anger and aversion as a source of energy to create something good or remove bad things from our lives. For example, the hatred of bigotry is one of the reasons this book was written. Hate is not purely negative when we properly direct it, understand it and use it.

To put it in simpler terms we must control our hate, not be controlled by it.

If we are going to make good use of the hatred we were given, we must never direct it at people. That leads to violence, intolerance, war, destruction and estrangement. That is the bane of mankind. We must learn to direct it at the actions of people instead of at people themselves. If we can learn to hate undesirable behaviors rather than people, the result will help us grow.

Now that we've seen the potential for such a negative emotion to have a potentially positive outcome, perhaps we can consider other simple truths to see if they contain benefit.

Pain is yet another facet of life many of us find difficult to deal with. In its purest form, pain is merely information. Pain lets us know when something is wrong. When things hurt, we avoid them. Such as fire. It burns, so we don't touch it with our bare hands. Pain also instructs us when we have reached our limits. Pain can be caused by exercising our muscles, for example. The result of that pain is our body sending more resources to those areas in which pain has occurred. This in turn promotes muscular growth. The sensation of pain is avoided by humans on an instinctual level but, as has been proven through the life experience of many, pain taken in the right way allows us to become more than we are. "No pain, no gain", right? A great many people spend their life avoiding pain because they fear it. Of course, there is nothing to gain from meaningless pain, but in moderation pain can do us a lot of good. Pain, like hatred, is not an evil. To inflict needless pain on someone else without a just reason is.

There are times when the only way to heal a broken bone is to break it again in order to set it correctly. That pain is necessary for the healing process. It is up to the knowledgeable and wise to determine when such a pain is necessary. A person who takes it upon themselves to decide when pain is necessary for others must be extremely cautious. It is far easier to inflict pain on someone than to have someone else inflict pain on us. We should be considerate of others when considering the benefits of pain.

Another simple truth: We experience emotional pain.

Understanding emotional pain becomes very complicated based on circumstances and past experiences. What pains one person emotionally may not give pain to another. Sometimes emotional pain is caused by attachment to someone or something and then losing that person or thing. Sometimes emotional pain is caused by the rudeness of others or by our own failures. Remember: pain is information. Remembering pain can help us to avoid making the same mistakes. It can also encourage us to build stronger relationships with those around us.

You cannot apply the same principles about physical pain to emotional pain. Physical injury and emotional injury are not healed by the same thing. One relies on the body, the other on the mind. We should respect the pain of others. Have you ever had someone brush your pain off as unimportant or unreasonable? It doesn't feel good, does it? Even worse is when someone brushes our pain off as necessary and therefore not deserving of compassion. That sort of thinking seems very likely to breed estrangement and weaken our society, not strengthen it.

Emotionally, a person must be allowed to heal on their own, for that is where the strength of the mind is gained. If we support those around us who are in pain, our relationships grow. If a person seeks help, they should have it. That is the nature of compassion. However, forcing help can be traumatizing. If you've ever seen a child try to walk, they try to do it on their own after a time because that is the only way to grow. They will push your hands away if you try to take away their struggle to stay upright. That's because forcing help will not help them to walk on their own. With emotional pain, we go through the same process. When it is new and overwhelming, we seek help. When we want to become stronger than our pain we have to do it on our own. It is up to the wise and empathetic to determine when a person needs emotional support and when they do not. A person who takes it upon themselves to heal the emotional wounds of others must be extremely cautious. Otherwise, we increase the emotional distance between ourselves and those we help.

So, we have taken two typically negatively viewed things, hate and pain, and seen how they can be beneficial to us. That kind of thinking is how we need to approach religion and faith. A "nothing is purely negative" will help us cultivate greater understanding.

Fate vs. Drive

One of the many concepts inherent in some religions is the idea of "God's Plan". This concept has endured great scrutiny over the years. The idea of fate is both encouraging and despairing at the same time for many. Fate is defined as that which is inevitably predetermined. (Dictionary.com, Fate) In other words: the unavoidable outcome of events often considered prescribed. Conceptually, fate is laid forth intentionally for reasons unknown by a powerful entity and for many that can be quite upsetting. No one likes to feel that all the misery and suffering in their lives was forced upon them by some intelligent and powerful entity. Neither does anyone like to feel like they have no free will. However, I for one don't believe in The Great Tyrannical Bully.

On the flip side, sometimes we are gladdened that good things are bound for us by "fate" and it can be encouraging that we cannot avoid wonderful outcomes. Of course, when we assume that, regardless of our actions, we will gain great wealth, prosperity, etc. we suddenly seem less accountable for our actions.

The conceptual problem with fate has several layers that need to be unpeeled if we are to understand it and accept it.

Firstly, when considering predetermined misery, we may ask what kind of God is just that delivers pain and suffering to us. If God is benevolent or just and all powerful, then God could not give us misery, pain or suffering that does not lead us to some form of improvement in the world. That would contradict God's benevolence or justness. It could be supposed that our misery occurs for the greater good, and that the benevolence we speak of is part of a larger plan, but then we ask why, if God is all powerful, should misery or pain happen at all? Can't God cause the improvement without the pain and suffering? All of existence is subject to God's will, after all.

The second issue arises with the consideration of free will. If our fate is predetermined, then free will is an illusion. We were always going to make the choices we made, and will make a specific set of choices in the future. Nothing happens that is not a part of God's plan so we really have no choice at all. Since there is no other alternative for action within this conception of fate, how could we be held accountable for our actions if we were always predetermined to take those actions? That doesn't make sense either.

In much the same way this issue comes into contact within the study of science. So far as mankind is aware, everything follows a set of laws. If you consider existence as nothing but pieces interacting under predetermined laws, including the very electrons in your brain, your brain pathways, cell structures, etc. then it seems reasonable to conclude that a human is bound to make the decisions it makes based on the chemical material properties that comprise the person and the universe that surrounds it. Therefore, again, we have to conclude that humans are scientifically predetermined to take specific actions and therefore there should be no accountability for a person's actions.

Considering the first issue: what kind of benevolent God intentionally gives us pain and misery when all of those things are within God's power to avoid? Considering the second issue of free will and fate, once accountability is removed the notion of good and evil falls to pieces and we are left only with a very rigid, unyielding structure for reality that we call fate.

So how can man have free will, accountability, and yet still be a part of a divine plan? That is the great question. If we are going to believe in God's plan and free will at the same time, we might start by observing something very small. The fate and life of a person is best described much like the path of an electron within the structure of an atom.

In the current study of electrons within the structure of an atom, the understanding is that there is a cloud surrounding the nucleus of the atom in which the electron exists at any given time. The electron moves so quickly it is difficult to say with certainty that the electron is in any given location at a point in time. The electron follows a path within the cloud. However, the electron is bound to that cloud. It does not leave that orbit around the nucleus unless processes such as molecular bonds forming or the atom becoming an ion occur, etc.

Considering fate in geometric terms, a line very poorly represents the life and fate of a person if we are to consider free will. If God's plan is a fate we cannot hope to escape (and thus our actions are predetermined), then a line with a beginning point and an end point would be an accurate representation.

If we consider our lives to be made up of a myriad of choices made freely, such as with free will, then our lives more closely resemble that of the electron cloud. There are many possible places our life may go, just like the electron. However, we only occupy one point in that cloud at any given time. The path our lives take within that cloud would be dependent on our choices, as well as our environment. For example, if we choose not to get out of bed one day rather than getting up and going to work, the trajectory of our life might change. If even larger decisions are made, then our trajectory changes more dramatically.

The reason our lives are like a cloud and not an

infinite span is due to the fact that there are places and things an individual will never do. The instant a person enters this world, the beginning point of their path through life is established. A person born in Africa, example, will not be in North America one second after its birth. Likewise, a person raised in a Buddhist culture will most likely never become the Catholic Pope. There are limiting factors of our lives which are determined by the world we are born into and cannot be changed by the choices we deliberately make.

    That being said, the possibilities within our lives produced by free will can take us to very extreme places, or very simple places. They all lie within the cloud in which our lives roam.

    Our environment plays a particularly large role within this illustration of free will. Just because we make a choice does not mean that our lives will assume the trajectory we desire. It simply means that we will veer in a certain direction. Therefore, where our lives end is determined by two factors: Our current path and our current drive.

    If a person has a strong drive to become a good person, stumble as they might, they will trend in that direction with each choice they make. The environment might make that drive easy, or difficult to realize, and thus the path might lead them closely in the direction they desire, or it may lead them away from that direction completely, or somewhere in between.

    The end point of the life we live within that cloud is not typically determined by us. Short of suicide (a very selfish act), a person does not typically decide when they die. A person might be driven to reach a certain state such as married with children in Vienna. They may even be on that trajectory, but environmental factors may end that journey early such as by a plane crash, or some other mortal interruption. Different decisions might influence when we die, but ultimately we die, and that always determines the end point of our life.

So, our beginning point is the place and time and from whom we are born. The end point is our death. The fate cloud is made up of all possible places we may end up based on our choices and our drive.

When we throw other people into the mix and consider interacting fates, what we see seems more like atoms forming molecules. Some atoms will interact with each other, and some won't. Some of those interactions will have a great impact on the trajectory of our lives, and some won't. If we step back far enough, with each life currently in existence represented as an atom, the multitude of human fate looks like a much larger amount of molecules, perhaps even an organism. In that way, fate lives and breathes, moves and responds.

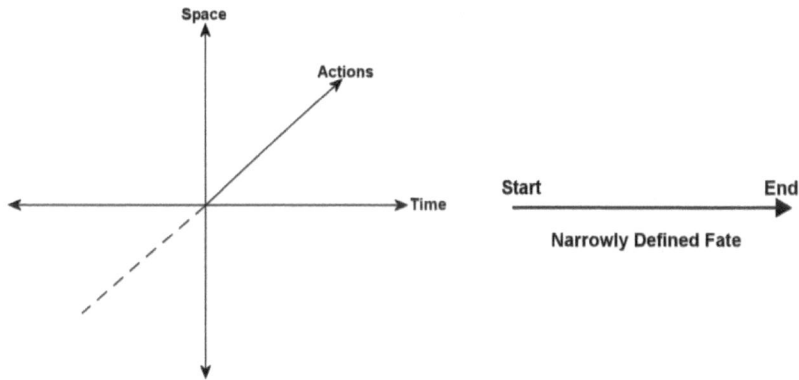

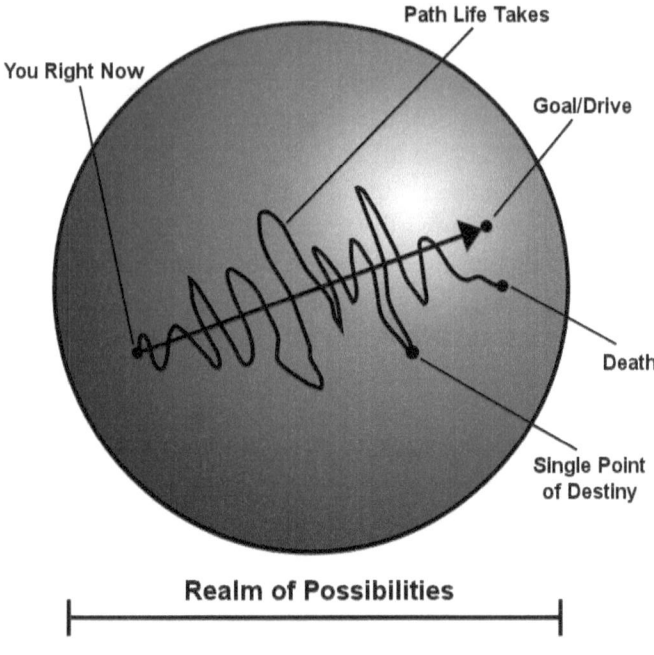

Fate vs. Drive

Now, if we consider a living breathing organism of possibilities and certainties, we can consider God's plan. Suppose that there are certain points within the possibilities of the fate organism that God has intended. Such a point might exist within the area of multiple people's fate clouds. Because of the interactive nature of humanity as a society, if one person decides not to do a thing, that doesn't mean that the thing will not be done. If God intends for a person to write a bible, for example, it may not happen because Joe decided to write it, because he chose not to, but John or Jacob might write it because that was their choice as well. It seems reasonable that while God won't force a person to do something (overwriting free will), God might nudge people toward different paths in that direction so that the point God intended within that fate organism is reached. As you can see by this example, those points of God's intent would represent God's plan, even within a world with free will. In this sense it is less of a micromanaging God achieving results.

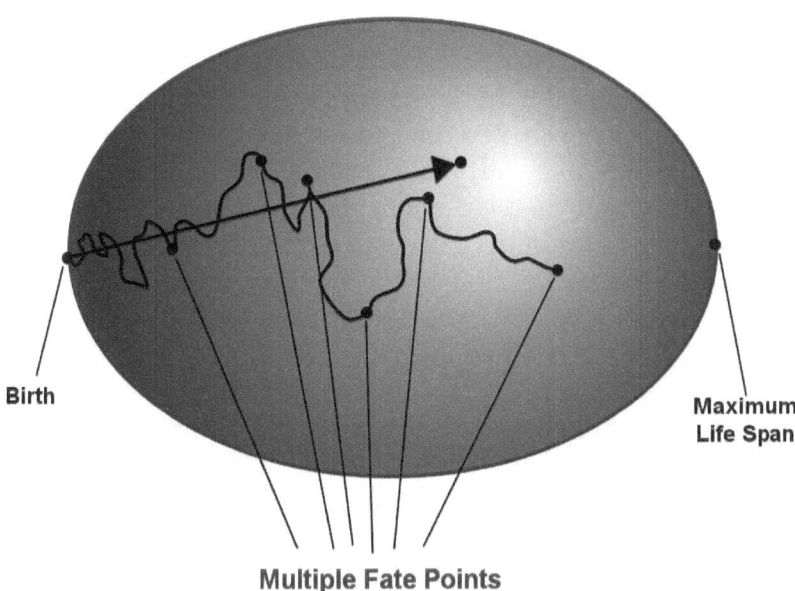

Multiple Fate Points

Let's take away divinity for a moment, and consider a more scientific approach to free will. Scientific study currently follows the theory that there are immutable laws which govern all parts and pieces of existence. In this view our fate is predetermined because our molecules and other particles must obey those laws, and cannot act in any other way. Gravity happens, which keeps us on earth. Combustion happens because of friction and energy. Natural response occurs which causes us to run from a fire due to the wiring of the brain. Procreation happens likewise, and so on etc. Until every "choice" made is merely an expression of the laws that govern reality. This view denies free will, and thus accountability for action, and therefor the concepts of good and evil. Evil is defined as being selfish, destructive and, most importantly, deliberately chosen. When free will is denied, so too is the latter of the traits that define evil, and therefore there can be no evil. Furthermore, without evil, good has little meaning.

That is a very narrow view of existence.

A simple truth: All that governs reality is not currently known. No one has determined concretely every law that governs this world. As such it is reasonable to believe that there are rules and laws that are beyond our current understanding. If there are things beyond our understanding, then it is possible that there are truths which allow for the idea of free will within the context of scientific law.

There are several possibilities that support the notion of free will within the realm of science, a few of which are included here and more than likely there are more that my limited understanding could not imagine. These are only possibilities, of course, not facts. However, their inclusion speaks on many levels to the true depth and beauty of science, as well as the possibilities of a reality in which free will is possible and is inclusive of current scientific theory. For the most part, these arguments would appear to correspond to the electrical signals traveling through the brain that create thought, which many would consider to be most important essential within the essence of free choice and reason. If this is truly where our wills are expressed, then in order for us to allow for the concept of free will, it must be proven that thoughts are not the result of a specific set of conditions that allow only for one result. They must allow for multiple results. So, if our thoughts are electrical signals governed by the laws of physics, we must find reasonable explanations within those laws that would allow for free thought, and thus free choice. Given some consideration, there could be several possible explanations. These are just the few my limited mind has come up with.

1.   Scientists search for laws and rules that govern the smallest particles that make up existence. Each particle gets categorized based on the properties therein such as quarks and gluons etc. As we look closer and closer into what makes up each particle in existence, we look at what those particles are made of. We look at smaller and smaller pieces hoping to find that base particle that makes up everything.

So, what if the smallest particles that make up everything are not identical? What if the smallest particles are all similar, but not the same? If this were the case, the laws that govern reality would govern all particles in a similar manner, but not always in the same manner. Sort of like how two particles cannot occupy the same space. If all the properties of the smallest particle(s) were identical, that might include where in space/time a particle exists, thereby every particle in the world could/would occupy the same space if on the smallest scale all particles of a particular kind were the same. In other words, if the properties of base particles were the same, that could mean that the x, y and z coordinates in space were the same as well. However, particles do not occupy the same space, so the idea that base particles are only similar but not the same is possible. This would allow room for variance within the reactions between particles, such as the trajectory of those little electrons. That little room we have just hypothesized for variances within the smallest particles in turn would allow for random events, since all base particles don't react identically, only similarly. That variable reaction, on a much larger scale as we look at larger and larger particles, would allow for thoughts and behaviors to vary not just based on environmental conditions, but on the principle that thoughts and behaviors do not fall on specific points, but on a range of points (kind of like our electron cloud), generating reasonable, yet unique results. In the realm of decision making, this could be enough to justify a free will.

2.   What if there were times, places or conditions in which certain laws of the universe did not apply? If there were instances where the laws that govern reality simply did not hold then the universe would be truly unpredictable. It would stand to reason that where the laws of physics do apply, the universe would be very predictable, but where they did not apply, true random events would occur. Those places where laws do not apply could be as vast as black holes, but potentially those places could exist at the subatomic level, allowing again for random thought. Random thought liberates the constrictions on choice, thus allowing for free will.

3.   If the laws of physics, on the smallest of scales, were not rigid values, but instead a range of possible values, this too would allow for free will. Joe is not limited to thinking that the sun is bright, but that the sun is very bright, horribly bright, searingly bright, or just a little brighter than normal, for instance. Again, we have variation within a set of values, for the sun still appears bright to Joe.

4.   While we narrow-mindedly search for the laws which govern reality, we must consider another possibility within our search which might seem absurd. We must consider the possibility that not everything is governed by laws. That is to say that when we search for an unknown we must consider the possibility that it does not exist. Historically speaking, it is like the search for the philosopher's stone. During the time of alchemy it was believed that there was a stone which allowed for the transmutation of lead into gold, and could also grant a person immortality. Just because we searched for it didn't mean that the stone actually existed. Not to say that there is no such thing as the laws of physics, but merely that there may be laws we hope exist that do not. Perhaps the smallest of particles does not follow laws at all, but merely acts

spontaneously. No doubt such a concept would baffle any scientist, and certainly anyone who has a firm belief in science who reads this will laugh at this conjecture. However, if we are to avoid foolishness, we ought to consider the possibility that our current beliefs and knowledge are wrong. Thus, though it is probably not true, consider the possibility that there are things in the universe that do not conform to the laws of physics. If that were the case, then random events are possible, and the idea of free will could come to fruition, much like those reasons listed above.

5. Another popular idea with current scientific understanding is that of alternate realities. If perhaps free will did exist, that gives rise to the potential for an individual to make many different decisions instead of just one. The concept of an alternate reality or realities is that whenever a person is confronted with a decision in which the choice is not obvious (such as choosing between two equally disliked colors) an alternate reality is created where the thing that wasn't chosen in this reality was chosen in the other. When you consider the number of decisions a single person makes daily, and the number of dilemmas that follow each decision an individual makes, quite a few realities would be created in just the single lifespan of one person. With the number of living people on the planet alone this exponentially increases the number of decisions made, and that's just considering the present day. Add onto that the number of lives before this very moment and suddenly the number of alternate realities that could exist becomes seemingly infinite.

This idea already considers free will a reality. Without the concept of free will, the notion of alternate realities falls to pieces.

These are just some possibilities, some or many of

which could be disproved. There are most likely more reasons besides what has been written here. The point of talking about these possibilities is to consider the potential for free will within the realms of science. Science searches for the same thing religion does, after all, and that is truth. If a true faith is to be developed, it must include truth. Without truth, we are left with little more than madness. Therefore we cannot discount science in our search for truth. It is feasible that free will exists even within the realms of science, and therefore the notion of good and evil, for if there is free will then we can be held accountable for our actions.

    I believe we are free from God's will. God may influence what choices are available to us but it is always our choice to make and that is the way we are intended to live. We are free from obligation and we are free to choose. We can choose to honor the path of righteousness and surely that is the best way.

    The fact that humanity has concocted such an idea as alternate realities and flexible laws is encouraging, for that is precisely the kind of open minded thinking which supports the search for truth. When we close our mind to possibilities that are beyond our capacity to prove, we shut the door on the search for truth. We could never have learned that the philosopher's stone did not exist had we not searched in vain for it in the first place. A large part of discerning truth is revealing those things which are false. Remember, a true faith does not accept blindly, nor does it ignore the wisdom of reason. It searches for truth with an open mind.

Humanity's Knowledge

"The scientist's religious feeling takes the form of a rapturous amazement at the harmony of natural law, which reveals an intelligence of such superiority that, in comparison with it, all the systematic thinking of human beings is an utterly insignificant reflection. This feeling is the guiding principle of his/her life and work."   -Albert Einstein

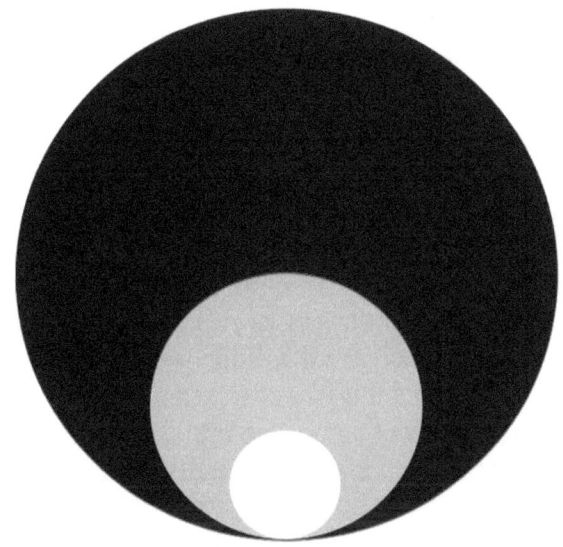

In the context of bigotry as well as foundational principles, often we come across the discussion of mankind's knowledge. A bigot often truly believes that they know the truth and that their knowledge is superior to all others. A religious bigot might insist that they have been endowed with knowledge from scriptures or some other form of religious education. In terms of the foundations of religious knowledge, we operate on the assumption that we possess knowledge of the universe and how it functions as well as spiritual knowledge. Knowledge is a sticky subject within philosophical discussion due to its perceived nature as the culmination of sensory experience and logical reasoning supported by physical evidence. So let's take a look at knowledge and perhaps we'll see why it can be such a sticky topic.

Knowledge is clear and certain mental apprehension as well as a perception of truth. The famous philosopher Descartes once wrote a philosophical work in which he argued that the only thing a human may prove and therefore truly know is that he/she exists either as real or as a deceived thing. You may have heard it as the simplified argument "I think, therefore I am". Because we can perceive things through our senses does not imply truth. It merely implies that we are perceiving something. As an example, one common affliction for people who have lost a limb is the sensory experience that the limb is still attached. This is called "phantom limb syndrome". Even though there is no limb to feel the senses still perceive it. In this example, perception contradicts supposed truth.

What is interesting about Descartes' work is that it is written in three distinct parts. The first two are probably most commonly talked about. In the first part Descartes argues that nothing can be proven to exist. In the second he argues that a human can prove to his/herself that he/she exists. There is a third, lesser known part, which deserves note. After arguing for human existence, Descartes strives to prove that God exists. This is striking in that a man who is certainly skeptical and seeking knowledge who uses logic and reasoning to philosophize still strove to identify God. What's more, his arguments bears a striking similarity to the Hindu concept of Maya or the illusion of what we know of as reality.

Maya is the idea that truth is perceived differently than it is. The easiest example is that of a rope laying on the ground in a poorly lit room. The viewer perceives that the rope is actually a snake even though it is still just a rope. At that time two things are perceived: The truth of the rope and the illusion of the snake. Both are a part of reality but one is illusion and one is truth.

"When one regards the creation as a fact and seeks its cause, Vedanta [Hindu scripture] formulates the theory of maya. From the causal standpoint maya, or the creative power, inheres in Brahman [God]. Maya is cosmic ignorance, under whose spell Brahman appears as the Creator, the individual ego, and the manifold universe." (Upanishads Vol 2 259)

This relates to Descartes argument for "God" because in his argumentation there is a thing which is or is not deceived that we call man, and there is a deceiver that deceives man that one could refer to as the guiding force of the universe. This force that influences the perception of mankind could be called God. In both Descartes philosophy and the concept of Maya there is the idea of what is believed to be known but that knowledge is illusory.

Taking the next step, we can see that the universe is both creation and creator combined.

"Some of those who regard the creation as real ascribe it to God's will. God, to them, is like a potter, who, prior to the creation of the pot, conceives its name and form in his mind. The creation cannot be unrelated or external to God's mind."

(Upanishads Vol 2 235)

The creation described relates back to the earlier musing we had over existence that God is in a sense everything. If all there was is God then the only material God had to create the universe was God's self. So while the universe exists, it is a part of God but not necessarily the whole of God. Like a cell by itself is not the body but a part of it. Which in turn relates to the following:

"… the universe is not a chaos but a cosmos. Brahman is its ground in the sense that the rope is the ground of the illusory snake. The appearance of the world does not effect any change in Brahman Itself."

(Upanishads Vol 2 18)

Based on the existential philosophy above as well as our own human experiences, it is reasonable to come to a conclusion that perhaps we could have explained more simply: Humankind does not know everything there is to know. Roughly five hundred years ago humanity knew that the earth was the center of the universe. Thousands of years ago humanity knew that the earth was flat. Imagine what humanity will say they "know" in the centuries to come.

At the beginning of this section is an image of a large black circle with a gray one within it and a white circle within the gray circle. This image serves two purposes, the first related to a potential view of existence in the context of creator and creation, and the second related to mankind's knowledge of existence.

In regards to creator and creation, one can consider that mankind occupies the white circle and that all of existence, including God occupies the black circle. In this sense, Mankind is a part of God, (lies within God) but does not make up all that is God, like the cell of a body related to the body itself. Thus, we can remember that we are a part of creation and yet we are not all that constitutes creation.

With regard to mankind's knowledge, humanity's knowledge is represented by the white circle. This is what human kind cumulatively knows about the truth of existence. Notice it is not even close in size to the whole of existence as depicted by the black circle. Next is the gray circle, which represents all that humankind will ever know about the nature of the universe. Our perception of existence is limited by our senses which are based on a physical world of matter. One could easily argue that mankind is simply not capable of knowing or studying everything in the universe. One could relate this to the Superstring Theory partially developed by Michael Greenand and John Schwarz in the early 1980's that poses that there are ten dimensions to the universe. We currently perceive four of those ten dimensions. Imagine if you will a two dimensional being. The universe they are aware of and can observe only lies in those two dimensions. The two dimensional being may theorize about the mysterious third dimension, but because the two dimensional being is limited to those two dimensions it cannot truly know that third dimension. In that same way, humankind may theorize about other dimensions but with the limitations of our four dimensional bodies we are likely unable to ever know those other six dimensions. In that way, mankind's knowledge will never exceed the gray circle, which although it is greater than our current knowledge it is still dramatically smaller than the knowledge of all that is, represented by the black circle.

So, when a person affirms that they know the way things are, such as that religious truth has been imparted upon them via scripture which was written by mankind, it is reasonable to question the validity of that statement. The simple truth is: Mankind does not know everything. Therefore we should be open to the consideration of ideas outside our own, be they religious or otherwise.

The following excerpt from The Upanishads illustrates this point particularly well.

"Before the advent of modern science the ethical laws in the West were largely determined by religion. Their sanction was derived either from tradition or scripture or from the words of a prophet. Most people lived an ethical life either from hope of reward or from fear of punishment, or from both. But today science dominates Western thinking. It has acquired its immense prestige partly for having invented what is called the scientific method and partly for promoting the physical happiness of man through the development of technology. Now, science has shaken the foundations of traditional religion by denying the existence of super-sensuous sources of knowledge. Such supra-mental realities as God, the soul, and immortality are not encountered by physical scientists in their pursuit of knowledge. But these very concepts have been the basis of traditional moral law.

Science seeks to give a new definition of morality, and in this it is largely influenced by the science of biology. According to biologists survival for an individual living being or for a particular living species is "good." Whatever is conducive to the continuous survival of that particular individual or species is therefore good for it. All this is implicit in the Darwinian theory of evolution. Struggle for existence, in which the fittest come out victorious, is one of the methods of survival. But it may give rise to a crude view of ethics, which has been called "gladiatorial" ethics. This method operates to a great extent in the world of animals and plants. The wars of modern times, fought with barbarous ferocity through the help of weapons invented by science, for the sake of national victory, make it obvious that human beings have not discarded the method of exterminating their competitors as a means to their own survival. But humane biologists point out another secret of survival, namely, adaptation and adjustment to environmental conditions. This too is a method of evolution. The individual or group that can adjust itself harmoniously to other individuals or groups has a better chance of survival than the one acting in a hostile manner. Hence the conduct is good which is conducive to harmonious adjustment to the environment. Biologists thus give a scientific explanation of the golden rule, which, according to them, need not be held to be derived from a divine source. The purpose of ethics is therefore to promote relationships between individuals and groups which are mutually satisfying. General survival is the goal which moral philosophers should never lose sight of. Without it there cannot be any progress in civilization or culture.

This view of ethics, however, can scarcely be said to give all-round satisfaction. The scientists deny the existence of the soul. They do not believe in a mind apart from the physiological functioning of the brain. Therefore the meaning of individual survival is not quite clear. Further, a group may, for its survival, co-operate with another group (or groups) possessing common interests, and enter into competition with outer groups having dissimilar interests. Thus the world becomes divided into hostile camps or blocs. The result is usually war, which – under modern conditions – can exterminate all. Mere survival, without higher values, may thus not be a desirable thing in itself.

The idea of progress, emphasized by modern science, takes it for granted that good and evil are two utterly dissimilar entities, and further that the former can be multiplied infinitely and the latter gradually minimized. The proponents of progress uphold the view that by means of scientific and other forms of knowledge man will be able to create a society from which evil will be totally eliminated. Does this goal envisaged by optimists possess a philosophical basis or is it mere wishful thinking? History does not prove that humanity as a whole and in all respects is on the road to the elimination of evil, ignorance, superstition, and misery. According to the Hindu view, the relative world is supported by the twin pillars of good and evil, pain and pleasure, and the other pairs of opposites. The sum total of happiness and unhappiness does not change. Evil, like chronic rheumatism, shifts from one place to another. World movements do not reveal progress, but simply change, as though in a kaleidoscope. Creation itself is an indication of lost balance. Where there is perfect balance there is no creation. The world will always remain imperfect. Perfection is to be sought elsewhere – outside the time-space continuum.

Moral life cannot be dissociated from struggle – an

incessant struggle for perfection, for the realization of the ideal, which, however, cannot be attained on the normal plane. It has already been stated that "oughtness" is the very essence of morality. But there lies a contradiction in the concept of morality itself. Since the moral life is a struggle of good against evil, it belongs to the realm of imperfection or relativity. No one can ever become moral and at the same time perfect. "Where there is no imperfection," as Bradley says, "there is no ought, where there is no ought, there is no morality; where there is no self-contradiction, there is no ought. The ought is a self-contradiction." Struggle through contradiction is the very basis of morality."(Upanishads Vol 2 30)

    This passage sums up well the relationship of science and religion, morals and survival. We are caught in a struggle to make good choices, much like we discussed with regards to fate and accountability of action. Without the possibility of free will there is no such thing as evil. And yet we perceive evil. So who is really to say which belief is right, or which one is wrong?

"Gibbons mate with gibbons. Deer mingle with deer. Mudsuckers carouse with mudsuckers. Humans consider Lady Feather and Deer-Grace the most beautiful of women. But if fish saw them, they'd head for deep water. If birds saw them, they'd scatter into azure depths. If deer saw them, they'd go bounding away. So of these four, which knows the truth about beauty for all beneath heaven?"
    (Chuang Tzu 28)

    As mentioned before, the goal of this writing is to stimulate thought of a spiritual nature, which inevitably includes the nature of existence as well as the concept of knowledge, be it spiritual or otherwise. To truly cultivate a worthwhile faith it is important to acknowledge that we don't know as much as we'd like to think. One human does not know as much as humanity as a whole knows, which is very little in the grand scheme of things. However, if we do not take the time to develop a strong and worthwhile faith, there is little point in "knowing" anything.

As we delve into the nature of morality and ethical behaviors, as is the nature of religious/spiritual discussion, we should keep in mind that there are things we don't know and there are perspectives we've never seen from. We should also keep in mind the simple things we see commonly as truth, for that is where a greater sense of knowledge can be derived. This is the surest way to avoid ignorance and eliminate bigotry.

Non-believers

"The Supreme Intelligence has granted man a huge treasury of spiritual and intellectual gifts, but none is more precious than the knowledge that God is infinite, both in existence and in wisdom, while man is as limited in his ability to comprehend as he is in his physical existence."

"… In other words, an essential component of wisdom is the knowledge that man's failure to understand truth does not make it untrue."

(Stone Edition Chumash, Numbers 19)

There are, in many holy books, verses that state that anyone who does not believe in that particular religious belief will go to hell or some other form of everlasting suffering after their death. In short, if you don't believe in a specific faith, you are damned. Below for example:

"And whoso believeth not in me, and is not baptized, shall be damned." (Smith 58)

Personally, I do not think this is right. You are welcome to disagree if you so wish, but please consider this: If God is omnipotent and all powerful as well as just/benevolent, then the idea that you will go to hell due to your spiritual beliefs contains a logical fallacy.

There are people in this world currently, and there have been throughout history in the various places of the world, who will never or have never had the opportunity to interact with Christianity or Islam or Hinduism etc. So, using Christianity as an example, if a person is born and lives a life and dies in a foreign country and never so much as hears of Christianity they will go to Hell as per the above assumption. However, if God creates all people, is omniscient and all powerful, this means that God created these people knowing that they would never have that opportunity to learn of the only faith that grants one access to heaven and knowing that they would therefore be damned by God's laws. If that is the case, one can infer that in this example, God created people for the specific purpose (since God is omnipotent and all omniscient) of going to Hell. This does not seem like a just or benevolent God.

A similar concept arises when we consider those who lived before the conception of a religion. Christianity was not the first religion. Neither was Judaism. Evidence of human presence spanning back as far as twenty five thousand years ago (or more) has been discovered in the shape of cave paintings and ancient instruments such as drums and flutes. Those people had never heard of Jesus. He hadn't been born yet. Nor could they have known about the Muhammad. Had these people also been created only to be damned? That doesn't sound benevolent or just either.

A person might argue that it is therefore the responsibility of the members of a religion to visit every country and every person to convert them to the proper belief. If that were true, it implies that God has purposely damned billions of humans throughout the ages since all religions have not always been in existence and that the purpose of a good believer is to convert everyone to that belief. That seems like an awful lot of damnation just to unify a people. The ends do not justify the means (though many would like to contend that they do). Justifying the means by the ends is the same as justifying evil. Evil leads to destruction, not salvation. Humanity has discovered this time and time again through millennia of experience. That is the nature of the universe. A God who wants us to convert everyone to a single religion such as Christianity is also not just or benevolent since the means to accomplish this includes the damnation of billions who have been purposefully created to that end with no chance of salvation. The ends do not justify the means, and God is supposed to be just.

It stands to reason then, that it is not the particular belief of an individual that grants them grace or bestows upon them damnation, but rather the actions of that individual. If that were the case, the practice of conversion is unnecessary. Only the teachings of doing good and avoiding bad would hold true.

There is truth out there with regards to the spiritual nature of existence. Perhaps it is our duty to discover it. Or, perhaps it is our duty to live a good life free from malice and destruction. Either way, based on the logical fallacy of belief based damnation, it is clear that one's beliefs are not the cause of damnation. It stands more to reason that there is something else that determines who is worthy of paradise and who is not. I suspect it is our actions and not our allegiance to a specific religion.

In addition to belief-based damnation, another interesting concept arises with damnation based on the acceptance of prophets as manifestations of god and following those prophets. That's not to say that Jesus or

Muhammad or Gandhi or any other prominent religious figures are not manifestations of God. It is to say that following those manifestations and believing in them is not necessarily the only path to salvation.

"Therefore everyone who hears these words of mine and puts them into practice is like a wise man who built his house on the rock. The rain came down, the streams rose, and the winds blew and beat against that house; yet it did not fall, because it had its foundation on the rock. But everyone who hears these words of mine and does not put them into practice is like a foolish man who built his house on the sand. The rain came down, the streams rose, and the winds blew and beat against that house, and it fell with a great crash." (International Bible, Matthew. 7:14-24)

The fact is that not every person on this planet will personally meet a living prophet in their lifetime. Furthermore, humans are often skeptical by nature and desire proof before they believe in something. God made us that way. The words of men are imperfect as mankind is considered by many to be flawed. Therefore, not everyone on the planet will properly receive the word of God through rhetoric or direct experience with a prophet. We have already discussed how someone having a specific belief versus another faith most likely does not condemn one to hell since a just God does not needlessly damn people to hell knowingly and intentionally. Nor does God create people in situations where it is completely impossible to make good choices and become worthwhile people. In the same way it can be argued that since mankind was made to be skeptical to some degree and since not everyone will have direct contact with a prophet that there must be other criteria for salvation. Therefore the necessary guidance a person needs to attain spiritual growth can be found outside of prophets and religion.

One could believe in one prophet, or many, listen to their words as well as believe in their Godly manifestation.

Or not. It is reasonable to believe, to that end, that God left his instructions to a good and worthwhile life through the properties and tendencies naturally found in existence. Those instructions are taught us by the consequences of our actions and the benefits and downfalls our actions cultivate.

    In a way, it would be better to have no spiritual belief at all if it was the only way to avoid conflict and bloodshed. There are plenty of people who do not believe in a higher power who are doing their best to live a good and worthwhile life. Additionally, one can believe in a higher power without causing such harm. Many have done so already.

    We have yet to form a culture conducive to good behavior and spiritual belief for all.

Prayer

Do you really think we must close our eyes to pray?
Does God want us to shut our eyes merely to express our devotion?
With our heads downcast, our eyes bathed in darkness and our hands firmly clasped,
are we any closer to realizing the truth that is the greatness of God?
God gave us eyes that we may see
whether in prayer or not.
We close them to block out the world around us
or because in the darkness we somehow feel closer to God.
I keep my eyes open, as a reminder to myself
that ignorance is the result of a lack of observation
and the shadow cast by an ill-used mind.
Open your eyes that you may not follow blindly
and walk steadily in the light of the lord,
instead of the obscurity of a darkened prayer.

A lot of religions the world over hold dear the time honored practice of prayer. Prayer is the act of expressing one's faith by means of confessing and/or asking something of a higher power as well as the exaltation of that higher power. People pray for a myriad of reasons. Some better than others, be it the salvation of a lost soul or the success of a winning lottery ticket.

In the New Testament, Jesus talks a lot about the art of prayer. (International Bible, MAT, 6:5-15) At the time people were making a big show of praying in order to demonstrate that their faith was strong and that they were righteous people. They were doing it as a show of status, trying hard to best their neighbor in how devout they were. Jesus knew that this was foolish and not true to faith at all. If we are praying so that others will see us pray, that is prideful and self-centered, which won't make us any closer to God, but further away. If we are praying to show how strong our faith is, then our faith must be weak since it requires the approval of others to be strong.

The reason we pray is the desire for a connection with the powers that be. Whether we are hoping to gain some benefit from God or simply because we believe that our prayer makes us beloved in God's eyes, the intent is a form of connection. When we are younger, we pray for things like wealth and luck, or a boyfriend/girlfriend or lover, or anything we believe will make us happy as we struggle in our world of turmoil. For those who grow wiser in their beliefs, we begin to pray for guidance in making our decisions and the wisdom to deal with the problems at hand. Sometimes we even pray because we simply love God. (Stone Edition Chumash, Deuteronomy 5, 29)

The nature of prayer is that it strengthens us when we start to analyze what it is we are praying for. When we pray for material things, very rarely will we get them. When we pray for our problems to vanish, they rarely do. All we have done with our prayer is taken the time to connect with God, acknowledge that our problems are there, or that we desire those material goods. The benefit of prayer in that respect is taking the time to allow us to express what strikes our hearts at that moment. The important part about prayer is the connection with God.

In an amusing example we pray "God please grant me whatever I desire." And God says "Certainly. I will remove from you your desire, therefore all you desire you will already have." When we pray for material things, we rarely get them. That's God's way of saying "no."

There are some things that are completely beyond our control. For example, during a natural disaster, we cannot prevent the flood or the volcano from erupting. We pray that God will have mercy on us so that the flood or volcano won't kill us.

When we pray for God to solve all of our problems, if those prayers were answered, it would make life easy and we would not grow. If we are to grow stronger, then it seems that we are meant to overcome our own obstacles that we are capable of dealing with. It is when we cannot possibly overcome obstacles that we pray for divine intervention. This is a very humbling prayer.

Making a habit of being in constant communion with God keeps us humble and helps develop our spiritual qualities. That is one reason it is good to pray often.

However, all things should be taken in moderation.

Praying every single night, while devoted, does not necessarily improve the quality of our prayer or increase the benefits of prayer. It may dilute it. Prayer without meaning isn't prayer, it's pointless speech or thought. Prayer without faith is hollow. It is little more than words without meaning. It's just noise.

As we continue to perform the act of prayer repeatedly, it starts to lose its meaning. It's like when you repeat the same word over and over again until it stops meaning anything and simply becomes a noise. That's not to say that a person can't pray every day and not have meaning in their prayers. It is simply that when we pray needlessly, we aren't strengthening the connection we seek with God. By making it numbingly repetitive we are only making it weaker. We should know when we need to pray instead of making it part of an obligatory routine. The conversation with God is unending and is never forgotten. We may think that a new day and a new prayer is the start of a new conversation, but we have always been in God's company. The conversation merely continues. To converse in this way is to maintain a constant connection with God.

    The best prayers are those felt with the heart where we reach out for God because we are deeply moved to do so. Those prayers are not made in familiarity, they are not obligatory, but are made in true desire for a connection with God.

    Many people may disagree with these contentions and perhaps they aren't true for everyone. Prayer benefits the person praying, surely. However, for the religiously blind, constant routine prayer that is a memorization and repetition only serves to perpetuate the blindness instead of awakening a strong faith. Speak with God. God listens. Regurgitate and you will upset your stomach.

    So what is it we should pray for? Material goods and things our hearts desire are often not what is best for us. Very few of us have a good sense of what is best for us. Winning the lottery, for example, probably won't enrich our lives but nurture our greed and laziness. It is doubtful that winning the lottery lies along the search for truth and goodness. Praying for ease in our lives does little for our resilience as a species. We all experience difficulties in life. Wishing them away will only allow us to grow weak. After all, we are made stronger by the obstacles we face. Praying for wisdom in the decisions we make is certainly something we all could use. Many decisions are difficult, and wouldn't it be great if we could make all the right choices in life according to God's will? Certainly we should try to gain wisdom on our own, rather than having it given to us. That said, mistakes help us to grow. The development of wisdom is paramount to living a fulfilling life and making this world a better place, and it is gained through struggle and experience. And mistakes.

One thing that is definitely worth praying for is to pray for guidance and pray for God to lead you to the path so that you yourself can walk it. We often get lost and aren't sure where we stand or where we should be going like in the swamp. At the least, if we can find our way back to the path, we can continue to live the life we were meant to. That is what it means to trust in God. It'd be nice if we always knew exactly what decisions to make, but at the very least we need to know what decisions are available to us and what kind of person God wants us to become in this world. Praying for guidance gives us that little light that helps us see the path ahead.

Of course, some would contend that God wants us to become someone very specific. That we should be obedient subservient creatures in God's world. That just sounds like bad parenting. Rather than a narrow rigid form of life, perhaps we should simply become someone worthy of praise for our good deeds. A good parent wants for their child to be good and successful. That is much better than parents who demand their children become doctors or farmers. Those kinds of parents have rebellious children.

The greatest means of becoming that person and walking the path we need to travel to reach that goal is through meaningful prayer. When a person can acknowledge that they are not on the path they need to be on, they are expressing the utmost humility when they pray because they are performing it not for the benefit of those who watch, but for their own sake in God's eyes. That is an acknowledgment that we don't know all the answers and that we have made and will make mistakes. That kind of

prayer puts us in God's hands.
    When we pray, perhaps we should pray for the benefit of all and the will necessary to walk the path we were meant to. Life is hard. Sometimes we feel like giving up. If God grants us strength, we can overcome our obstacles and grow.

Speak,
With the words God has given you,
As spoken before and will again,
That your soul may ignite
and be a lantern in this world.
Speak silently those words
that they fall gently in the wind.
Each word in eternity echoes,
resonating,
until each ripple grows and shakes and builds
into a roaring cacophony that rumbles in the bones
and sings softly upon the heart
How can such harmony help
but to tremble in the deep and crumble the mighty peaks
and raise the masses into a resounding shout
"Hallelujah!"
Speak, my friend,
though the melody seems to fade,
for it will linger in its time,
and whether hidden or seen
will gather you home
though you may have lost your way.
Speak, dear soul
For God has given you voice.

Right and Wrong

Good vs. Evil

  A bigot believes that they know what is right and what is wrong with absolute certainty. They know it only from their personal point of view and lack the understanding of other viewpoints. Without an all-encompassing understanding, a bigot lives in ignorance. They do not know what they are struggling against and do not understand the impact of their own actions. Yet they continue to fight. A bigot in religious terms believes fully that they are fighting for the greater good. The bigot desires good outcomes. Their battle is one for benefit. However, it is not a battle they can win.

  Sun Tzu said it best when he said "if you know the enemy and know yourself, you need not fear the result of a hundred battles. If you know yourself but not the enemy, for every victory gained you will also suffer a defeat. If you know neither the enemy nor yourself, you will succumb in every battle."(Sun Tzu 15)

  A bigot has already lost the battle for the greater good because a bigot's actions push people away from the bigot's opinions and create hatred and estrangement. Nobody likes being told that they are wrong or that their viewpoints are worthless. Why would anyone want to listen to someone who stubbornly insists that only they are right? In the spiritual sense, if we are going to create a world in which bigotry cannot flourish or grow, then we must have an understanding of basic things that humankind views as evil and those things we view as good. We must understand what makes those things evil, as well as where those things might not be evil. Taking the viewpoint that "nothing is purely negative" we must look for the positive within the negative if we are to gain true understanding. If we have a full understanding of the way we should live then we do not speak in ignorance and can understand the viewpoints of others. If everyone developed this way there would be no room for bigotry.

Each religion I explore boasts many beliefs about the spiritual world and moral behavior and each religion is different in many ways. However, there are many commonalities between them. More specifically, most religions seem to agree that there are certain things that should be done and certain things that shouldn't be done. Even outside of the doctrine of religions, most people feel innately that there are certain things that should be done and shouldn't be done. Take for example: Murder. Most people agree that it is not something that should be done. Another example: charity. Most people agree that it is something that is good to do. So, when unraveling the philosophy of a good faith, it seems reasonable to believe: Regardless of the particulars of religion, there are certain actions a person should not take and there are certain actions a person should take. This is the essence of right and wrong.

The presence and assumption of such a thing as good also suggests such a thing as evil. Considering the presence of evil, it becomes important to determine if there is a purpose to evil or not. After all, God created all things. So, is there such a thing as a necessary evil? There are some who believe that good cannot exist without evil, nor evil without good. This premise implies that evil is necessary. I personally do not believe this. I believe that humanity should strive toward a better world which cannot exist without the mitigation of evil. Evil exists, certainly, but it is not necessary. I can imagine an existence without evil, and it is an end worth striving for.

Good and evil are often set up as a dichotomy, but in doing so we don't leave room for any gray areas which prevents us from truly understanding ourselves and the world around us. Dichotomies are an either/or organization of concepts; Right or wrong, good or bad, strong or weak, light or dark. The fact is, we operate in the in-between places. There are acts of evil that have good benefits, and acts intended for good that cause harm. Light and dark aren't the only options. They are options, but it is between them that the visible world exists. If there was nothing but light, we wouldn't be able to see since it would be too bright. If there were nothing but dark, we wouldn't see either. If there was nothing but only light or dark, we'd still see only nothing. It is in places that are darker than light but lighter than darkness that we are capable of perceiving, metaphorically speaking.

If we're going to understand the gray areas in between "good and evil", we have to understand what makes something evil, and what makes something good. So, how do we define evil? How do we define good? There are characteristics that must be present for a thing to truly be evil. There are characteristics that must be present for a thing to be good, and furthermore without those defining characteristics, a thing is neither good or bad. It simply is.

Evil is defined in many different ways by many different people but when we look at commonalities between evil acts it becomes apparent what traits define it.

Some religions give homage to the figure called the devil, or Satan; an otherwise evil deific presence that leads men astray. In my mind there is no such thing. You are welcome to disagree. God created all things, sure. Even the temptations we face. However, one can contend that evil does not dwell with such deific power at its command. Mankind seems incapable of taking responsibility for its own misdeeds. That is human nature. We are ashamed of our mistakes and so in some instances we will say "The devil made me do it" and "I was possessed by a demon" in order to place the blame on anything other than ourselves. Does that seem like taking responsibility?

I have never seen anything in my short walk on this our earth that makes me believe that evil is a presence apart from us or deific in nature. I have only seen evidence of this: Evil comes from the hearts of human kind.

"… This is the mischief of the slinking Devil, who comes stealthily and casts evil suggestions into the hearts of men. The whispering of the evil one is the greatest mischief because its source is in the hearts of men." (Stone Edition Chumash, 1260 note 6a)

It is mankind that commits atrocities, injustices and falsehoods. A tree is not capable, nor an instinctual creature, of committing sin. Perhaps I am wrong. However, I would challenge anyone to show me an evil pine tree.

To define further the concept of an evil entity, I would like to draw attention to responsibility. It seems to me that whenever a person makes a mistake or commits some act of indecency, the person or perhaps other people sympathetic to that person claim that they were tempted by the devil, or possessed by a demon, or led astray by Satan. I feel that this is an excuse and not a reason. Instead of blaming our faults on anything but ourselves, we should take responsibility for our actions. We are not perfect beings. We will make mistakes sometimes. We will succumb to weakness once in a while. Everyone does at some point. However, instead of blaming it on things external to ourselves, we should acknowledge our mistakes and misdeeds, learn from them, and resolve to be stronger and not do the same thing again. Using the devil as a crutch to divert the blame becomes a weakness. Being strong and responsible; This is a good way to go about doing things. That is why I do not believe in the devil.

So what separates mankind from the animals? This argument is a frustrating one at best and I have met a fair few who come up with unprovable reasons that animals do or do not have souls and so forth. I won't get into those arguments because I do not possess the ability to prove that animals do or do not. Many argue about whether or not animals have souls, about why humans and animals are the same or why they are not. Often the argument stems from the concerns regarding whether or not it is moral to kill or harm an animal. Regardless of the outcome of such arguments, there is something of importance to note when we look at animals as opposed to humans, and that is the concept of choice.

There is a parable about a scorpion and a coyote that illustrates something fundamental about free will. The story goes something like this:

There once was a scorpion who wished to cross a river to reach the plentiful food on the other side. The scorpion was trying to figure out how to get across when a coyote happened by. The coyote also wished to cross the river to reach the plentiful food on the other side. The coyote was about to enter the water to swim across when the scorpion spoke up.

"Coyote." Said the scorpion. "I see that you are going to swim across the river. Would you please let me ride on your back so that I too may cross it?"

The coyote thought about the scorpion's request, and considered it for a moment. "If I do that, you'll sting me." He said.

"Why would I do that?" Asked the scorpion. "If I sting you while I'm on your back, we'll both drown in the river and neither of us would reach the other side. I have no interest in drowning."

The coyote considered what the scorpion had said and found no flaw in the scorpion's reasoning. "Very well. Get on my back and I will take you across."

When the coyote had swam halfway across the river, the scorpion stung him.

The coyote cried out in pain and began to sink in the

river. "Why did you sting me?" He said, "Now neither of us will reach the other side and we'll both drown."

"I'm sorry." The scorpion said. "It's in my nature."

The message of the story, ultimately, is about the nature of a creature. Bees sting, wolves eat and birds fly. What separates the creatures in this story from humans in nature is mankind's ability to defy our own nature. To put it another way, we can resist our instinct and act on our intellect to make choices that are many things but instinctual.

Why is it a man can commit evil, but a lion cannot? It is the ability to defy that instinct. Both compassion (as illustrated by the coyote) and natural urges (illustrated by the scorpion) are instinctual. Many animals in this world experience compassion. That is why you might see a cat raising a puppy.

Humans can not only defy our compassion (especially for each other), and make hard choices like choosing who should live and who should die, but we can also defy our natural urges, and abstain from sex or fast instead of eating when we are hungry.

We expect a wolf to eat when it is hungry and a sheep to flee when a wolf is nearby. That is their nature. The sheep will always choose to flee, and the wolf to eat. That is not choice, but the natural flow of the world.

Humans have a choice. We can choose to give in to our impulses, to help or harm based on the emotions we feel. We can also rely on our logic and intellect to act beyond our impulses. To forgive a murderer for their crimes, or to seek justice instead of vengeance for those we have lost.

The truth becomes plain when we acknowledge the presence of choice when defining good and evil. So what is Evil?

Evil is an intentional decision to take an action that is both selfish and destructive. Evil is made self-evident by the destruction it causes to us, others or the world around us, be it directly or indirectly, obvious or subtle.

The nature of evil isn't always obvious, but the misery it creates is. When a person takes things from others for his own benefit, it is to the detriment of those he stole from. When a person kills another for revenge, the family of the victim is filled with pain and anger, perhaps seeking vengeance upon the killer. Situations can be simpler than these, or more complicated, but the outcome is the same: A selfish action causes destructive results.

Selfishness is the attempt to separate one's self from the rest of the world. When we are truly selfish we try to be like God and possess and control all that we can, thinking that we alone are important. However, no one person is that great. When we are selfish we forget that we are a very small part of a very large whole. To become God in ourselves we would have to remove ourselves from the body that is the all encompassing God. By removing ourselves from all that is we kill ourselves, like a wart being removed from the flesh. A wart is only a small part of the body. Once it has been separated it dies. The wart cannot survive without the body but the body can survive without the wart. Mankind cannot survive without God but God can survive without mankind. Evil makes us wither and harm the world around us. When we harm the world around us we are malignant. Malignant things are best gotten rid of, like a tumor. Shouldn't we live in such a way that we are not best gotten rid of? If we live in harmony with the whole and recognize that we are only an insignificant part, then we can live selflessly and the body can thrive.

Some forms of destruction are not as apparent as a person dying or people being sad. Some evil influences a person or society in a negative way. For example, in choosing to be lazy and forsake our duties, we encourage a society where that kind of sloth is acceptable and even expected. Our actions are observed by others and, whether we like it or not, those who observe us our are influenced by what we do. Those influenced may seek the outcome of our own laziness or imitate our laziness. If we overvalue goods and see that stealing is a way to gain wealth, we may begin to steal. Without good effort, people tend to be selfish. Evil is not always obvious or simple. That is where the gray areas need careful consideration. If it is not readily apparent what damage is caused by an action then it falls on us to delve into the repercussions of our actions to determine if something is truly destructive or not. This is where humanity often falls short and why we should seek greater understanding.

      Let's take a moment to clarify destruction. When I refer to destruction in the context of "sin" in the contents of this work, I am not referring to destroying a building, or destroying bad things, nor am I referring to destructive processes like nuclear fission. Destruction in the context of morality means to reduce to useless pieces, a useless form or remains by rending, burning or dissolving; to injure beyond repair or renewal; demolish; ruin; annihilate.(Dictionary.com Destroy) For the purposes of sinful action, destruction refers to the unnecessary physical, psychological or social injury or ruin or death of the self or another person or animal, the ruin or annihilation of a nurturing group of people or society, and the ruin beyond repair of ecosystems and species beyond the human race including plants and animals. The ruin of a nurturing group comes in the form of habits, customs and behaviors that increase the amount of destructive behaviors within the group, the estrangement of members of a group and the corruption of the nurturing elements within a group. Sometimes destroying a building is of benefit to the society that built it. Sometimes destroying elemental bonds adds to the amount of knowledge man has of physical science. Destroying bad things removes them from society. Destruction itself is not evil. Things get destroyed. For the rest of this document, let's use this definition of destruction with regards to "sin" for the purpose of greater understanding.

    If God created everything and gave us free will, then it almost seems like a great experiment of sorts. God has set the variables (us and our free will) and God has set the parameters (our environment and the consequences our actions bring). The parameters are unchanging. Things like where we live, what the world is like and so forth, the natural laws (such as gravity) and the consequences of our actions are all parameters. The only variable is free will, and everything acts in accordance with it. A man is made angry when the woman he loves sleeps with another man. That is part of the parameters. It is his choice to do or not do something about it that is the variable.

    The analogy of an experiment isn't perfect, but the point it illustrates about the nature of free will and choice, as well as by the consequences thereof is important. We have the choice to take the easy route, to give in to selfish action. The parameters of this world tell us it is not a wise decision to act selfishly due to the destruction it causes which we as a people have learned from experience, but even so humans make those choices anyway. This is the fight between good and evil.

    Cultures that revolve around lust, greed and pride have happened throughout the ages. Unfortunately, America is one of those cultures and the amount of crime, violence and irresponsibility in this country is staggering. While it isn't necessarily the result of one person's selfishness, the damage caused is undeniable. That is the culture we have created. Because the consequences aren't obvious, it becomes difficult for people to see where we've gone wrong.

Another simple truth: Each of us is free to do as we wish. It is our choice to do the right thing or not and we have the right to make that choice. No one can take that away. We may face consequences for our choices but the presence of choice is irrevocable.

So, for now, let's keep our definitions simple. Evil is an action both destructive and selfish that is willingly and intentionally chosen by an individual. Evil is self-evident by the destruction it causes to us, others or the world around us. We are taught the wrongness of Evil action by the misery it creates.

Qualifying Evil

Many people have heard of "the seven deadly sins". Some religions incorporate it into their doctrine, some do not. I bring mention of it here because there is some truth behind this notion that evil can be categorized. Categorization helps us to understand and recognize evil. These categories are only useful to that end and many evils are a combination or indistinction between different categories but at the source they all share the same common factors: Selfishness, intention and destruction. I won't call them deadly sins, for many things are deadly, but I would call them evil nonetheless. I would argue, however, that there are more than seven. Opinions on what is evil and what is not vary from religion to religion, but these are the things that mankind seems to agree are the basis of evil in our world. Each of them is tied together by commonalities. Those choices we call evil are all destructive (physically, emotionally and intrinsically), intentional, and they all revolve around selfish desires.

When we do something that isn't selfish, though it may be intentional and destructive, it is difficult to really call it evil. If we were trying to do something because of someone else's desires, is it really something we should be held accountable for? In ignorance maybe.

When we do something selfish and accidentally cause destruction, can we really be held accountable? We should certainly try not to make the same mistake in the future, but we really can't be blamed for an accident. That's why it is called an accident.

When we purposefully do something for selfish reasons but nobody and nothing is harmed, who can call that evil? All voluntary actions arise from ourselves, even if it is from our desire to help others. So long as no one is harmed and nothing is ruined, why should it matter? Keeping in mind that destruction isn't always physical injury, of course.

When we deliberately do something to harm or hurt because we want to satisfy our desires, we have placed ourselves above the welfare of things greater than ourselves. This is the path of ruin. If everyone acted in this way, we certainly wouldn't have a society like the one we see today.

"People of the world, being weak in virtue, engage in strife over matters that are not urgent. In the midst of abject wickedness and extreme afflictions they painstakingly toil for their living. Whether noble or corrupt, rich or poor, young or old, male or female, all people worry about wealth and property. In this there is no difference between rich and poor; both have their anxieties. Groaning in dejection and sorrow, they pile up thoughts of anguish or, driven by inner urges, they run wildly in all directions and thus have no time for peace and rest." (Kyokai 47)

"... The second evil is that people of this world – parents, children, brothers and sisters, family members, husbands and wives – all lack moral principles, break laws, conduct themselves arrogantly, commit licentious and unruly acts, pursue their own pleasures, enjoy themselves as they will, and deceive each other. What they think contradicts what they say; they speak without sincerity, flatter others with deceitful intention, fawn upon others with artful words, envy the reputation of sages, abuse the virtuous, and entrap people by dishonest means." (Kyokai 55)

"... The third evil is this. People of the world live together inhabiting this realm between heaven and earth, with a limited lifespan. On the one hand, among the higher levels there are wise, rich, honorable, noble, and wealthy people. On the other hand, among the lower levels there are people who are poor debased, crude, and foolish. Besides, there are evildoers who always harbor vicious thoughts and think only of self-gratification; they are full of worries and sunk in lust and attachment; they are restless in their daily lives, greedy and miserly, and desirous of what they have no right to possess. They gloat over fair-skinned women, behave licentiously and commit obscene acts with them, hate their own wives, and secretly frequent brothels. Consequently, after squandering all their resources they begin to break the law. They form bands, start riots, engage in fighting, unlawfully attack and kill people, and plunder property.

"Some have evil designs on the possessions of others. Without working at their own occupations, they acquire things through theft. Driven by desire, they commit further offenses. Feverishly agitated, they intimidate and rob people to support their own wives and children with the goods thus acquired. Obeying only the dictates of their passions, they become addicted to wanton pleasures. They also disregard seniority in kinship, causing sorrow and anguish to other family members and relatives; furthermore, they take no account of the laws of the state."

(Kyokai 57)
"... Nevertheless, they expect good fortune and seek long lives, only to meet death in the end." (Kyokai 61)

This excerpt demonstrates the selfish tendencies of human beings and shows why developing moral foundational principles is so critical to our lives. While there are certainly a good many things a person can do that are viewed as sinful behaviors we need to learn to understand where those behaviors come from and how to overcome them. Let's look at these categories of destructive acts. Bare in mind that the purpose of delving into these concepts is to help foster a deeper understanding from a "nothing is purely negative" point of view. If we are going to stamp out bigotry, we must learn to see things from all angles. You may or may not agree with what I have said here, and that is fine. Surely I have not unraveled each of them fully and without error. I am merely trying to encourage productive thinking. Through better understanding we will be better equipped to face the obstacles in our lives.

The Ten Sins

Wrath

Wrath is vengeance or consequence as the result of anger. Wrath is evil when we take our anger out on something or someone. Our actions have consequence. That much is apparent. When vengeance or hateful action occurs without due cause it simply confuses us. When a dog is punished for peeing on the carpet, the purpose of the punishment is to train the dog not to do it. When a dog is punished because the owner was cheated on by his wife, that punishment doesn't accomplish anything. It simply makes the dog feel hated, worthless, and quite probably confused. The dog could have done nothing to prevent the adultery and in no way was responsible for it happening. The result is little more than destruction to the spirit of the dog and the relationship between the owner and the dog. There is nothing more confusing than suffering for something you didn't do wrong.

Another expression of wrath is when the consequences do not fit the offense. For example, if a guest purposefully spills a glass of wine on the carpet and the host beats the offender to the point he is put into a hospital, what has the host accomplished? The relationship between the host and the guest has been ruined, probably beyond repair. The behavior of spilling the wine might not happen again, but while the behavior may have been corrected, all that is left is an utterly destroyed relationship. If the host instead chides the guest who spilled the wine for ruining his carpet needlessly, the result is more equitable to the offense.

Similarly, when a thief is killed for stealing, society grows fearful and that fear leads to problems within the society. The thief should certainly learn not to steal, but killing him won't solve anything. It will make the thief's family upset and perhaps resentful or even vengeful. It might make the family seek out revenge for the lost family member. The punishment for stealing needs to fit the offense, and ideally encourage members of society not to steal, instead of simply making society afraid and perhaps resentful for the death it witnesses.

Wrath is typically an expression of our negative feelings. People in pain, people who have made mistakes or have experienced failures often take it out on the rest of the world. Even worse, those people who feel they need to control everything often lash out when things don't go their way. For example, a manager expecting to make sales when the economy is suffering takes it out on his employees when sales goals are not met by making them work twice as hard. It isn't the employees' fault that the surrounding population doesn't have the money to spend on their goods, and yet they suffer for it. Like the example with the dog, nothing is learned and nothing is gained. All that is accomplished by the wrath of the manager is pain and suffering. The only thing the manager gained was feeling like once again he was in control and in power, which is nothing more than selfish.

    We are wrathful when we consider ourselves more important than anything else and take our anger and frustration out on other people, creatures, or objects. Wrath results in misery and suffering and destroys our relationships with others. If our wrath is not taken out on others, it's taken out on the world around us and the result is the destruction of whatever happens to be in the way. Selfish, destructive, and a choice to express our anger physically or emotionally, wrath certainly fits the definition of evil.

    Anger and wrath are two different things. Certainly one leads to the other. Anger does not always lead to wrath. Anger is simply an emotion. In a way it gives us information. Anger encourages us to avoid the situations that make us angry. Now, in some cases loss of control can cause anger. Using anger to inform us that we simply must maintain control over everything at all times is not a very useful way to interpret that anger.

    Conversely, as an emotion, anger can give us great drive to act. When people are angry, they often take strong action to do something with that anger. The key to using our anger in a way that does not prove wrathful and destructive is to channel that anger into something else. Utilizing anger to provide the energy necessary to build a home, or to protect those we love is a wonderful way to turn away from wrath.

On a personal note, I use my anger at people who treat others poorly to strengthen my resolve to do right by others. The means to my revenge against those offenders is to live a good life and treat others with respect so that those who acted poorly and mistreated me will see that in spite of their best efforts, they have failed to bring me down. In that respect, anger is like a fuel.

It is acceptable for a person to experience anger. It is a natural emotion. It is not acceptable for a person to visit their wrath upon others.

Similar in its aggressive nature is hate.

Hatred is an intense dislike, extreme aversion or hostility. (Dictionary.com Hate) Hatred is viewed by many as an evil in and of itself but when fully explored we may find that hatred by itself is not evil. It is merely a negative emotion. When we hate things we avoid them or visit our wrath upon them.

Naturally, hatred can be a force that drives our wrath. Hatred toward an individual might cause us to lash out at that person needlessly. Hatred toward a culture or group of people can cause us to be discompassionate and disrespectful. However, hatred can also be a powerful force for good when it is directed at the right things. For example, when we hate bigotry we strive to make the world more tolerant (such as the contents of this book). When we hate violence we struggle for peace.

As an emotion, hatred is not inherently evil. It is when hatred drives our wrath or makes us discompassionate of others that it becomes a vehicle for destruction.

Lust

Lust is perhaps one of the most difficult topics to

talk about due to its intimate nature. Sex is best kept to the bedroom, as they say. Of course, we don't need to discuss the finer points of sex, but the topic of lust is of crucial importance to moral understanding. Everyone experiences sexual desire. It's part of human nature. Intercourse is necessary for the continuation of the species. That is a simple truth. When we talk about Lust, we aren't talking about procreation, however. To define it more precisely, lust is uncontrolled or illicit sexual desire or appetite. (Dictionary.com Lust) It isn't just a desire for sexual pleasure. Lust occurs when we cannot resist temptation and give into our desires.

  As a selfish act, lust is about experiencing sexual pleasure. In this respect it is similar to gluttony, as it is a desire for a sensory experience and it can become very addicting.("Clinical Management of Sex Addiction" 4) As an intentional act it isn't just the desire for sex. Lust is lust when we give into our desire and act upon it. As a destructive act, lust can destroy potentially positive relationships, it can destroy an individual's sense of intimacy, it can lower the value we have for our own bodies, and it can create a lack of compassion for others. Not to mention unwanted pregnancy which, for those unable to properly raise a child, often results in pain and suffering in the child's life.

  The more we indulge in sensory pleasure, the less impact it has. Take for example the rush of your first time running across the ground. The thrill of the wind on your face, the joy that you have discovered how to move quickly over land. Imagine the pride you felt when you accomplished enough physical coordination to run. Yet do you even remember the first time you ran? Do you still feel that same thrill? Of course not. I don't personally know anyone who does. The simple truth: The more you do something, the less it can mean to you and the less you might enjoy it. The solution to the problem of diminishing returns is equally simple: Moderation. Lust is one of those acts that needs to be controlled all the more. Otherwise, the idea of intimacy vanishes and we stop treating our own bodies as special. You only get one body, you may as well treat it well. So too for your partner.

With regards to relationships, consider this: You can love without sex and you can have sex without love. The two are not mutually dependent. I've seen many a relationship that were about nothing more than sexual desire, with very little in the way of a meaningful relationship. Those types of relationships tended to be disconnected and often abusive (physically or emotionally) in nature because love was not present. In those cases one or both partners were simply satisfying their desire for sexual pleasure.

Additionally, when sexual relationships outside of a compassionate relationship occur, it violates the sanctity of the compassionate relationship. It is a good thing to cherish your relationships. One way to ensure that your partner feels truly appreciated and special is to engage in monogamy. How wonderful it feels to know that you are the only one important enough to be trusted with your partner's body, and vice versa. Multi-partner sex relationships decay this special bond and ultimately result in jealousy, spite and a lack of compassion, which can also lead to abusive relationships. That is one of the reasons why polygamy has undergone such scrutiny in human history. We have had entire societies centered around the practice of polygamy and have since started to move away from the practice as a global culture. In the past perhaps we had reasons for the practice, which I will not argue here. Naturally, there will be some or many who disagree on the topic of polygamy and surely productive discussion should be had on the topic. I would, however, like to say this: Truly cherishing someone you wish to have children with is a good practice.

It is better to have one meaningful relationship than a thousand temporary ones that lead to pain. After struggling to find a meaningful relationship I have learned how disappointing it is to start relationship after relationship only to have the relationship fall apart, and that was without the allure of lust. Without self control over sexual impulses, I can only imagine a more painful life than I have experienced. If you treat your relationship as special, and do not share it with others outside your relationship, you will have a bond greater than any sex you could ever hope to have. The wise treasure the time and connection with another human being physically, mentally and emotionally. Only a fool squanders the sanctity of their relationships for temporary pleasure.

The worst expression of lust that you will see in the world is rape. Rape is a very difficult topic to discuss because it is a complete and utter violation of human trust, respect and dignity. To violate someone's body against their will is despicable and is on the same level of evil as murder in many a person's eye. Ask your friends and family what they think is worse: Rape or murder? Ask yourself the same question. With murder we are simply removing a life. With rape we create a world of shame, emotional pain and terror for someone. It is completely selfish to sacrifice someone else's dignity in order to experience pleasure. That is why society has such great penalties for rapists. Rape is also often not about sexual pleasure but about power as well. It disregards the victim as a person (apathy), places the rapist as greater than someone else (pride) and is sometimes realized as someone's punishment for someone else (wrath). As you can see, some things are not simply one small finite category of selfishness but rather a cumulative selfish act.

Lust is difficult to discuss because of how personal a matter our bodies are and if we aren't in control of our impulses the results destroy the quality of our lives. Does that mean we shouldn't have sex? Our species wouldn't last for very long if we didn't. Does it mean we can't enjoy sex? Surely not. Lust is the lack of control over our own desires for sexual pleasure, and unlike other sins, the intimacy and sanctity of human relationships is on the line. It is better to love without sex, than to have sex without love, and a truly wonderful relationship requires love to be fruitful. Lust is defined by the difference between the selfish desire for pleasure and the compassion for another person.

Sloth

Sloth is the habitual disinclination to exertion; indolence or laziness. (Dictionary.com Sloth) Sloth comes in several forms: The disinclination to physical action, the disinclination to thought and the disinclination to social interaction. Thinking, socializing and physical activity consume energy and, depending on the intensity, can potentially be exhausting. Laziness is in our nature. Why do something when we don't have to?

The consequences of physical inactivity can be obesity as well as atrophy. If a person is consistently inactive the body does not grow. It decays.

The consequences of avoiding mental exercise are ignorance and a feeble mind. If a person avoids taking the time to think, the mind does not grow. It decays.

The consequences of avoiding social interaction are detachment from our relationships and a lack of social skills. If a person does not take the time to socialize, the personality does not grow. It decays.

Of all the sins, fighting against our own sloth illustrates the ability to defy our instinct best. The reason sloth illustrates this best is because in order to defy instinct requires the understanding that our own atrophy is ruinous to a healthy and happy life. A person has to acknowledge that temporary satisfaction derived from inaction does not outweigh the benefit of hard work which results in growth. In order to see this, a person has to think about the consequences of the moment and the consequences in the future. Very few animals consider that their actions will affect a long term future. Most animals fulfill their instinct for the short term. A cat, for example, might give itself exercise because it is incapable of chasing down its dinner, but if it doesn't need to in order to eat it will become lazy and be in far poorer physical condition as a result. That's not to say that most animals don't live a happy and healthy life if left in the wild. They have to keep in shape and grow in order to survive. Our life is filled with obstacles, many of which are difficult to overcome. We grow by overcoming difficult situations. When we are slothful we take the easy route which is often harmful to ourselves and to others.

"… The fifth evil is this. People of the world are indecisive and slothful, reluctant to do good, lacking in self-discipline, and they do not work hard at their occupations; so their families and dependents are left to suffer from hunger and cold. When reproached by their parents, they retort angrily with scornful looks. In such conflicts they are far from peaceful; they can be as violent and frenzied as when enemies confront each other; as a result, parents wish that they had no children.

"In dealing with others, they are licentious and wayward, causing trouble and annoyance to many. Even when they are morally obliged to others, they neglect their duties and have no intention of repaying their indebtedness. Destitute and driven to the most desperate ends, they have no way of regaining their wealth. Although eager to obtain much profit and appropriate the riches of others, they waste their money on wanton pleasures. As this becomes a habit, they grow accustomed to acquiring property illegally and to spending their ill-gained profits on personal luxuries; indulging in wine and sumptuous food, they eat and drink to excess. Profligate and contentious as they are, they engage in foolish quarrels. Unable to understand others, they forcibly impose their will upon them.

"When they come upon people who are good, they hate and abuse them. Lacking morality and decorum, they do not reflect on their conduct, and so are presumptuous and insistent, refusing to take the advice and admonitions of others. They are unconcerned if their kinsmen, from the closest to the sixth blood relative, have no means of livelihood. They disregard their parents' benevolence and do not fulfill obligations to their teachers and friends. They think only of doing evil; their mouths continuously speak malice; and with their bodies they are forever committing evil. In their whole lives they do not do even one good deed." (Kyokai 59)

We as humans, with all our tools and knowledge, often need to do less in order to survive. The saying goes that "necessity is the mother of invention". In my humble opinion that saying is somewhat fallacious. I would contend that in large part laziness is the mother of invention. We don't need tools to survive, just like every other creature on the planet. That rules out necessity. It is a lot less work to use a tool to do something in order to survive, however. The only inventions that are created by necessity are those which are necessary to satisfy our intellect, not our survival.

Take transportation for example. We do not need transportation to survive. Humanity survived just fine prior to the invention of the horse and carriage, let alone the automobile. Transportation only served to allow us to go further faster and with less effort. It became necessary for the transportation of people and goods in order for us to build greater and greater societies, which is about the growth of humanity on an intellectual level, not necessity. We don't need transportation to gather food or shelter ourselves against the elements. We don't need transportation to protect us from predators. Thus, transportation was not created by necessity for survival.

One form of sloth is inaction within important circumstances. For example, if a plague were spreading in the east and the only way to stop it was to inform those who weren't infected before it reached them, inaction could result in thousands of deaths. When we are presented with the opportunity to do the right thing to help, save, or protect others, a failure to do so because it is difficult is no less a form of sloth.

Of the more common lazy behaviors you may see, I think the most striking is the decision not to call the police at the sound of a gunshot. This is called social inhibition. We think to ourselves "someone else will handle it" when that may not be the case. We might be the one person who makes that phone call. If we were the only person who might make that phone call and we don't, a person could die and the person who did the shooting may very well get away without consequence. This does not improve society nor does it help us hold ourselves accountable for our actions as a society. Not calling the police, in this instance, is sheer laziness. If we choose not to be lazy when we hear gunshots, the result is less injury, damage and crime.

An important distinction we need to make here is between sloth and rest. Rest is a time of inactivity in order to repair and rebuild the body or the mind. Social activities can be exhausting. We need time to recollect and reflect and grow from our social interactions. Physical activities on a small scale injure the body. We need time to repair our muscles and organs after physical activities. Thought can also be exhausting. We need time to process and make sense of our thoughts. Without resting the mind, people go mad. Rest is important. Sloth is unnecessary rest or inaction.

Pride

> "All men make mistakes, but a good man yields when he knows his course is wrong and repairs the evil. The only crime is pride."
> -Sophocles; Antigone

Before we talk about pride we have to make a distinction between pride and confidence. Many people are prideful and many are confident. Some are both. However, there is a large difference between pride and a knowledge of one's worth. This distinction points directly to why pride leads us to destruction. If we can understand how to be confident in ourselves without being prideful then we can achieve greatness.

Pride: A high or inordinate opinion of one's own dignity, merit, importance or superiority; whether as cherished in the mind or as displayed in one's bearing or conduct. (Dictionary.com Pride)

Confidence: Full trust; belief in the powers, trustworthiness or reliability in a person or thing. Belief in oneself and one's powers or abilities. (Dictionary.com Confidence)

In short, the difference between self-worth and self-importance is the difference between truth and selfishness. Pride comes into fruition when we believe ourselves, or something we hold to be important, to be better than something else. As C.S. Lewis said, "As long as you are proud, you cannot know God. A proud man is always looking down on things and people: And of course as long as you are looking down you cannot see something that is above you."

I once knew a man who was so certain of his own opinions of science and God that he refused to believe anything else. We'll call him Stan. Stan was convinced that his own opinion was worth more than anyone else's. He stated that in 2015 A.D. humanity would know all there is to know about the universe. It's 2017 and we're still learning things we never knew. With our thoughts and opinions, if we truly are to be humble, we have to assume that our thoughts and beliefs could very well be wrong. When we acknowledge that our thoughts and actions could be wrong, we open ourselves up to correction and the truth. If we do not, we become ignorant and prideful.

Pride, unlike self-confidence, leads us to put down the ideas of others. A surefire path to bigotry is that of pride. Humans put great stock in the things we believe we know. You will never hurt someone so deeply as to disprove something a person is proud of. Humans want to be important. We crave it. As Dale Carnegie will contend in How to Win Friends and Influence People, we crave importance more than anything else. (94)

Remember Stan? That same man who believed we would know everything by 2015 was also quite heartless in the name of his own pride. Once, at a game night when the players were enjoying a table-top roleplaying game, he insisted that the game master was incorrect on a mathematical point within the game. The point he was insisting on had little bearing on the game. Stan was insisting it would take less than a day of travel for the players to reach a certain point based on distance and speed. The game master had wanted it to take several days of travel for the players, regardless of the supposed distance in order to fulfill the flavor of the story she was trying to tell through the game. To her and the rest of us, it made little difference if it took the characters in the story three days of travel rather than the one. However, Stan wouldn't let it go. So he told the game master that she was wrong, which of course was a hurtful thing to do on such a petty point. She was starting to get upset so she told him to drop the point. He did not, and insisted again, this time more forcefully. She left the game (and us the players) upset and went upstairs. All of the players felt he was out of line, so we tried to explain how his conduct was wrong. He went so far as to insist that his conduct was perfectly fine because he had been right about the mathematical point he had contended, and furthermore that she shouldn't have been upset when he had told her how to run her game. Even after we explained that the game would not continue unless he went upstairs and apologized for his behavior, he would not budge. He went upstairs to tell her that he was sorry that she got upset. That was it. He wasn't sorry for acting the way he had or that he was out of line. He said he was sorry that she had gotten upset.

      This story illustrates the sort of evil pride brings. Stan was prideful of his opinion of what was important in the game we were playing. His selfishness caused him to damage the relationship between himself and not only the game master but the other players as well. He was even given the opportunity to admit his mistake and he would not take it because of his own feeling of self-worth. His personal importance was more important to him than his relationship with others. His behavior created hatred and estrangement in the group of friends all in the name of that self-importance.

Fame Vs. Personal Glory

      If we're going to talk about pride, let us look at the prideful nature of man in the popular venue of celebrity. You don't have to look far to find an actor or actress who treats everyone else like dirt because they feel more important than anyone else. That's the nature of celebrity. Sure, there are some celebrities who do not partake in selfish vanity, but the temptation is always there. We allow it to be. We want ourselves to be important, and we want to see ourselves in our celebrities, so we make them more important than they truly are. The result is unreasonable demands, selfish tempers and a slew of vain acts that we tolerate in the name of popular culture. It is perhaps one of the greatest flaws in American culture.

I'd like to point out another distinction as we continue to discuss pride regarding fame and personal glory. Fame is the recognition by the masses of an individual or group. Fame and the search for personal glory are not the same. Personal glory is what happens when an individual strives to be important. Fame happens when a person achieves excellence in some fashion. It is not wrong to achieve excellence. Excellence drives human progress. The search for personal glory only breeds vanity. If you want to be famous, you'll only be prideful. If you devote yourself to excellence, fame is the result. All the rest is the machinations of celebrity.

Elitism

"... Holding themselves in high esteem, they think that they are virtuous but act waywardly in an overbearing manner and despise others. Unaware of their own evil, they never feel ashamed of themselves." (Kyokai 58)

The greatest atrocity visited in the last thousand years was the result of pride. Not of an individual, but of an entire nation. So wretched and depraved was this act of pride that the nations of the world vowed "never again". I remember going to school and spending a good several weeks studying the Nazi holocaust. It sickened me on a level I have never since felt. There were a great many evils boiling around in the Nazi war machine, but the greatest of these was pride. The Nazi propaganda was strongest in the belief that German's were superior to every other country, and that the Arians were superior to every other race. Because of this feeling of self-worth, that nation rounded up groups of people and murdered them, experimented on them and in general disregarded the sanctity and rights of those people completely. All of this was the result of elitism. Elitism is the idea that a group or person is above everyone else because they possess specific traits. The truth is that in some ways perhaps that person or that group may be better, but it is impossible for a person or group to be better in every way. Especially since there will always be one way in which an elitist is inferior: Pride.

Elitism results in discrimination and the judgment of others. Elitism fosters hatred and estrangement. It is not our place to judge others. The only person we should ever be critical of is ourselves. The more we strive to correct our faults and develop our strengths with humility, the greater a person we can become.

Double Standards

One expression of pride is the famous double standard. A double standard is a standard that we apply to others but don't apply to ourselves, or vice versa. Another way of describing a double standard is hypocrisy. For example, if someone demands that others retain their virginity prior to marriage but engage in premarital sex themselves, that is a double standard. When such a thing occurs, it is because the person feels that they are the exception to the rule. They feel that they should not be held to the same standards because they are more important. Aggravating, isn't it, to be held to rules and regulations when someone else isn't?

So why do we always seem to blame others first instead of ourselves? Psychologists have been looking into the causes of this kind of behavior and what they've found is not a rule but a tendency. When people have shortcomings they tend to attribute the fault in favor of the self. This attribution comes in two forms. The first is the self-serving bias. That is, the tendency for a person to blame external sources more than the self when a mistake is made. It is hard to admit our mistakes so often we look for any reason that justifies our actions, rather than recognizing that we have shortcoming and have made a mistake. The second way people tend to assign blame is known as a fundamental attribution error. When we look at the behaviors of others, we have a tendency to blame the internal aspects of a person who has made a mistake more than we blame the external factors that may have caused them to make the mistake. This is where people often fall short in respecting others and being charitable to others. How often have you heard someone call someone else stupid when they made a simple mistake? In short, often when we are at fault we tend to blame everything but ourselves, and when others make mistakes we tend to place the blame on them instead of everything else. The truth lies somewhere in the middle.

    The blame game is of no benefit. When a problem arises, does blame solve the problem? Of course not. All blame does is make people feel bad or remove responsibility from someone who genuinely made a mistake. If you want to solve a problem, solve the problem. If a person has a shortcoming they need to be the one to recognize it and hopefully seek a means to correct it. If we decide to try to correct someone else we are placing ourselves above that person instead of allowing them to grow by learning from their own mistake. When we tell someone they're flawed, they tend to get upset. This is harmful to the relationship between us and that person and can negatively affect the social setting in which we operate. Most of the time, people are aware they made a mistake on some level be it consciously or subconsciously. When we focus on correcting the problem rather than assigning blame, the person who made the mistake typically realizes that extra effort is required to compensate for their mistake and they often already feel bad about it. Then they tend to self-correct over time. This is a much more positive way of helping others grow than making others bitter and upset because we've become prideful and focus on blaming others. Wouldn't you like to be treated that way?

    Taoist philosophy encourages us to clear the mind of the idea of self. "He considers those who point out his faults as his most benevolent teachers. He thinks of his enemy as the shadow that he himself casts."(Lao Tzu 61) When we forget the self, pride vanishes, and with it the damage it causes.

    Pride is what led the Nazi German's to commit countless atrocities. Pride is what makes the United States feel that it has the right to police the world. Pride can cause damage on even the grandest scales, which is why we should be ever humble and acknowledge our own shortcomings. Pride is not confidence. Confidence helps us keep in clear view our capabilities and helps us achieve excellence which is the driving force behind human achievement. Pride helps us destroy what is around us and is a driving force behind human misfortune.

Greed

"It is well known that a man earns money through untiring labor and great suffering yet does not derive from it enduring satisfaction."
                              (Upanishads Vol 1 128)

    Currently, greed is one of the greatest afflictions in the United States. Corporations seek money and power at the expense of the people who help them to secure it. Americans spend their lives struggling to become rich quick and to buy everything they've ever wanted. We consume more gasoline than any other nation, we bombard our citizens with advertisements for goods and we try to do as little as possible to gain as much as possible. That is the culture we have cultivated. The United States is only the most recent example. Greed has been at the core of many a great empire. The desire for unnecessary wealth beyond the needs of a person or country is what we mean when we talk about greed.

Greed has various shapes and sizes, but the core principles remain the same. Greed is the desire to possess things as well as the fear of losing those things. It takes the shape of hoarding, miserliness and theft. Does that mean is it a sin to have things? No, of course not. Everyone wants to have things, and many things we need if we are to live and accomplish great things in our lives. But again: moderation. If one person possesses everything, that leaves everyone else with nothing. If a person takes, there is someone (or something) it is taken from.

Greed as a desire for goods is an evil when expressed in a few particular ways. The first is when it leads us to do destructive things in order to obtain what we want. For example, killing someone so that we are the only inheritor to a large estate, or spreading lies to convince the governing authority that certain goods are ours instead of the rightful owner's. The second is when things are obtained to the detriment of others, such as acquiring all of the food while a village starves. The destructive potential for such an act is obvious.

Miserliness is the act of holding on tightly to goods and refusing to contribute one's wealth to others. Miserliness typically affects the surrounding environment little. However, the love of wealth is destructive to the person who typifies the behavior. The simplest and most renown of examples comes straight from The Bible: The parable of the talents.

The parable of talents is about two different cases of the use of one's wealth. It can be ascribed to a persons talents as well as a person's wealth, but for the sake of understanding we'll say it applies to wealth in this case. The story is about two men who are given a small sum of money. The first takes his money and buries it underground so that it will never be lost. The second takes his money and invests it in businesses. After a long period of time, the man who refused to utilize his money digs it up later and he has only what he started with. The other man has multiplied his wealth two fold because he used it to improve the economy. (International Bible, MAT, 23:14-30)

This example is an oversimplification, but the point I'm trying to make should be apparent. When we hold on to our wealth we are unable to use it to best effect to benefit people other than ourselves. Society typically will manage on its own without that wealth, but when you consider the impact such miserliness has on the miser it becomes apparent that the miser is not only a victim of his own fear and insecurity, but grows more dis-compassionate toward his fellow men. In this sense, greed turns into fear and dis-compassion (discussed later).

Another problem concerning the coveting of goods is that when things belonging to others are lost or stolen, those who lose their goods tend to get angry and seek retribution. A simple truth: people don't like it when you take their stuff. That's human nature. I personally find it preferable to live in a world where people aren't at each others throats all the time, and making people angry by taking their stuff is contrary to that purpose. I'd also prefer to live in a world where people aren't identified by what they own.

What about theft vs. possession? Do we really possess?

A person owns something when they have the means to secure it from others with their own strength, skill and cleverness. Of course, this implies that if it can be stolen then it isn't owned. People claim ownership of things they believe they have earned, things they have purchased, and things that have sentimental value, and occasionally things they simply want. However, wanting something doesn't mean that it belongs to us, neither does purchasing something. If a thing was stolen from one person and sold to another, the first person will still believe it belongs to them and if it was of great enough value they may try to get it back.

Philosophers may wonder if we truly possess. In as much as we define possession as I have above, certainly. In the sense that a thing is only ours, it can only be said that we own ourselves, for that is the one thing that cannot be taken away. The rest is external to the body, and removable. Sure, you can kill a person and claim that this "takes away that person from themselves" but that is foolish. You may gain power over an individual or their body, but it is still their body and ownership doesn't change, merely the physical state of that body. The nature of ownership of self is irrevocable. Goods, however, are revocable. We gain them by creating them out of the things around us and they can be stolen and returned by ourselves and others.

So, if possessions are defined as goods we can secure with our own strength, skill and cleverness, then do we possess? If we possess, we can dispossess. If we can dispossess, we can steal, and be stolen from.

This brings us to the difficulty of theft, and the all important question: Is theft wrong? To answer that, which can be a gray area, we must consider the reasons we steal. And there's a lot.

Why we steal:
- We want it

- We need it to survive (food, water, etc.)
- We need it as a means to another end (stealing a bike to escape the police)
- We want to keep things from the hands of others (like weapons or food)
- We are afraid to be without it (security, such as savings accounts)
- We want to give it to someone else
- We feel the owner is not deserving of it
- We intend to sell it for money for whatever end. (In this case it could be due to laziness or unwillingness to work for our livelihood or it could be due to needing money to legally obtain the things we want, etc.)
- Kleptomania (which should be noted as a mental disorder and therefor not part of healthy life)

So what of Robin Hood? Robin Hood is a story about a man who steals from the rich and gives to the poor. It is important to note that he stole from a corrupt and contemptible prince who was himself greedy in his taxation of the poor. So, Robin Hood was a thief. He stole. He stole from a thief. There's that retribution I mentioned earlier. Furthermore, we applaud Robin Hood for what he did. There is a big implication in that observation. Stealing is okay so long as it's from the rich? Perhaps not. Stealing from the corrupt? Perhaps so. It is also important to note that Robin Hood did not keep the money for his own selfish desires. He gave that money to people who were destitute. While I don't feel that we as a people should steal from the top one percent of wealthy people, at the same time, the greed from the top one percent can be detrimental to society. Personally, I think Robin Hood did a good thing by taking from the truly greedy to give to those who needed that money to survive in the world in which they were living.

In answer to the question: Should we steal? No. However, there are plenty who have succumbed to greed who are not deserving of what they possess. While the topic of judging others and enacting justice on those we feel are in the wrong is subject to a much larger debate, it is the responsibility of every person to curb their appetites for goods and to refrain from excess.

If nobody was overly greedy, people would not steal. There are plenty of resources to go around. It's therefore the responsibility of every breathing person on this planet to live in a way that promotes an environment without greed. This can be achieved by living a life where goods are obtained in moderation, not excess, and by striving for necessities instead of luxuries. I'm not saying we can't have frivolous things we enjoy like television or electric guitars or automobiles, but luxuries should be practical and in moderation, and necessities should be taken care of first and foremost. Owning seven cars is not practical, nor is it in moderation, nor is it necessary. Owning seven cars is a prime example of over-valuing goods and living in excess.

We desire goods. There's no way around that. It's in our nature. But we can strive to live in moderation, to own necessities and enjoy luxuries in a practical sense.

"When we overvalue goods, people begin to steal."
(Lao Tzu 3)

Greed is not simply owning or obtaining things, but a desire for things. I grew up in a society that more and more valued personal possessions and technology. While I don't feel that striving to own things is bad, I saw how this kind of culture affected people who did not possess the means to obtain the things they wanted.

Is it wrong to own things? No. We need equipment to create things, we need food to survive and we need shelter to protect us from the elements. It is plain that we cannot do without things. What we don't need is excess. A person does not need all of the highest end tools to create a simple tool shed. A family does not need enough food to feed a hundred people. A shelter that can house a hundred people is not necessary for a family of four. If you've ever read or seen the play "You Can't Take It With You" then perhaps you understand the fact that all the wealth we acquire through life does little good at the end of our days. The play is about a man who spends his whole life in business and as he has grown old his only real accomplishment is the wealth he's acquired much to the detriment of his family life. Wealth is nice to have, but in the end if we spend our lives acquiring and hoarding wealth all we've left behind is material goods. The world will be no better a place for it and our lives will have been meaningless. You can't take it with you. So why should we dedicate so much time and effort to it? Detachment from worldly goods is not about not having goods but instead not coveting, keeping or attaching ourselves to goods. It is easy to see that all goods perish, so losing them is insignificant.

Envy

Envy is a feeling of discontent or covetousness with regards to another's advantages, success, possessions, etc. (Dictionary.com Envy)

Jealousy is mental uneasiness from suspicion or fear of rivalry, unfaithfulness, etc. (Dictionary.com Jealousy)

You may hear some point out a distinction between envy and jealousy, but the fact remains that both are discontent with the self due to the desire for more than the self possesses. We are envious of the skill of others, the fame of others, the lives of others, the lovers of others. We become jealous because we feel that someone shouldn't be shared with others. We also become jealous because it hurts when the person we want to give us attention is giving that attention to someone else instead.

In some instances it is because we want to be better than others (see pride). In other instances it is because we simply want what we do not have (see greed). In some cases we are envious because we feel inferior. Regardless of the object of our envy, it stems from selfish desire.

    Before we can truly call it a sin, we have to understand the actions that make envy such a dangerous thing. The feeling of discontent or covetousness can be a strong driving force for self improvement. You will never find greater athletes than those who seek to be better than their opponents. The best of athletes focus on personal achievement of course, but in order to push ourselves to our limits we must have opposition and seek to surpass it. Our jealousy can drive us to make our relationships stronger and to treat those we love better. When we feel our lover is dissatisfied we may do something special to strengthen the bond with that person. These are not evil desires.

    Envy and jealousy become destructive only when they drive us to selfish action. A jealous lover is a dangerous thing. I've heard plenty of stories of abusive relationships because one partner is a jealous person. When a person decides to lash out at the object of their envy it becomes a problem.

    At one point in my life I became good friends with a co-worker of the opposite sex. She and I had been working together for over a year and enjoyed working together immensely. We were just friends, however. One day she asked me if I would like to hang out with her outside of work. I wondered if her husband would have a problem with it, but like a fool I assumed that she had already cleared it with him. It wasn't that she required his permission, but rather that she should ensure that he wouldn't be jealous if she spent time with another man. It's always a good idea to act in such a way that your partner has no reason to be suspicious or jealous.

We got together a couple of times to hang out, and that's all it ever was. I was not interested in her more than as a friend and I had no desire to dishonor the marriage of another person, let alone my good friend. After we got together a few times I received a message from her husband telling me with very harsh language to stay away from his wife.

Lesson learned on my part. I decided promptly that I would refrain from hanging out with her outside of work for the sake of her marriage. Like I said, I had made a foolish choice. Recognizing that, I did the right thing.

With me (the threat) out of the way, there should have been no problem. However, her husband's jealousy became unhinged. He began emotionally abusing her at home, yelling at her and threatening to dissolve their marriage. Additionally, he demanded that she not even so much as talk to me at work, or sit with me during our lunch break. Occasionally, he would stop in during her work shift at our lunch and when he discovered that we were having friendly conversations he would accuse her of being unfaithful and yell and scream at her.

As I said earlier, our friendship was just that: A friendship, nothing more. I never even made physical contact with her except for the occasional handshake or high five, but that didn't matter to him. His jealousy took control of his actions and he became a monster to his wife.

Jealousy is a two-way street. On the one hand, we should use our jealousy to treat our loved ones better rather than worse. On the other hand, we should do our best to give our loved one no reason to be jealous in the first place. If we fail to do this, the result is misery and suffering. On a small scale, jealousy leads us to petty actions and lashing out against those we care about. On a large scale, jealousy leads us to kill in the name of our own selfish desires. If we use jealousy to aid in our desire to love and keep our partner happy it can be a great strength. If we allow it to dominate our actions it can only do harm.

Envy of others is just as dangerous a desire. When a person is envious of another's possessions, the envious person could be led to steal or destroy the other person's possessions. When a person is envious of another person's success, they can be led to sabotage that person's success. Or even worse, to assault or kill that person. We all want to have good things and be successful. It's not wrong to strive for success nor is it wrong to obtain things. When we allow our envy to drive our actions we must be careful to keep it from being destructive.

I once knew a guy in high school who was very successful in the theatre. He was a decent actor, a hansom guy and beloved by the majority of the theatre crowd. Of course, I was envious. I wanted the attention he had, I wanted the success and the fame. However, rather than succumb to petty actions to bring him down from his pedestal (the notion of 'if I can't have it then nobody can') I strove to better myself instead. The action was certainly selfish. I drove myself to improve, to reach out for more prominent roles in plays and tried very hard to make a good impression with the theatre crowd for my own personal benefit. What I did was intentional, and certainly selfish, but the one thing it wasn't was destructive. What harm was done by striving to become a better actor? I suppose I spent a lot of time or effort but the result was self-improvement. What harm came from making a good impression with the theatre crowd? I made more friends and promoted a positive environment. The point I'm trying to make here was that although my envy was very real and I acted selfishly, I directed my desire toward a positive end rather than letting it drive me to hurt someone else.

Envy and jealousy are not in themselves destructive.

However, without proper self control they can bring us to cause great harm. Remember, in order for something to truly be considered evil, it must be three things: Selfish, intentional, and destructive. Jealousy shows us that we truly care about our relationship. Envy informs us of our desires. Both feelings can be redirected to promote beneficial results rather than destructive ones.

Gluttony

Gluttony differs from greed in that it is not what we possess that makes us gluttons but rather what we consume, be it food, substances or experiences. Gluttony is defined as excessive eating or drinking. (Dictionary.com Gluttony) Both of these acts are acts of consumption. If we look at gluttony as consumption it can be applied to things that are not food and drink, such as drugs or entertainment.

Let's talk about the consequences of gluttony as defined above for a moment. Some of the symptoms of gluttony are fairly obvious.

Obesity is perhaps the most common example of the consequences for being a gluttonous person. Some people overvalue the experience of eating. Modern science has proved that there are other factors that can cause obesity but obesity can certainly be a symptom of gluttony. People who are obese have more severe health problems than a healthy person such as heart attacks and joint problems.

If obesity is the most obvious, alcohol addiction is definitely the second most apparent symptom of excessive consumption. Alcohol addiction can result in severe health issues much like obesity can, but it can also result in damaged relationships and fractured family life. A simple truth: People who drink in excess tend to become unstable.

The damage that can be caused by addiction is not limited to alcohol, however. You don't have to go very far to find examples of drug addiction that have ruined lives.

Addiction is dangerous and incredibly difficult to cure. Look up any illegal substance such as methamphetamine or PCP and you're sure to run across the consequences of prolonged drug use. Drug abuse tends to result in a very poor quality of life, be it a life of poverty or a life filled with strained or broken relationships.

Substance abuse is also a waste of time, energy and resources. Drugs cost money, often a lot of money. The time people spend getting high could be used to greater effect in an almost endless list of potentially productive activities.

I once had a supervisor who would take a smoke break once every hour to every half hour. He would be outside the building smoking for a good five to ten minutes at a time. In the course of a single eight hour work day, on average he probably spent an hour and a half smoking. Sure, he was polluting his lungs. That is a health issue. It was his right to smoke but the amount of time he spent doing it was detrimental to his career as a supervisor. As a result the employees he supervised suffered due to his lack of supervision. He could have been much more productive as a supervisor if he hadn't been addicted to nicotine and had spent his time supervising his employees.

The last type of gluttony is far less obvious, and its consequences more subtle, but it is destructive nonetheless. This form of gluttony is the consumption of experiences, also known as hedonism. Hedonism is the devotion to pleasure as a way of life. In short: "If it feels good to do then do it". There are many people today in the United States who simply want to spend all their time having fun and doing what they want instead of building something worthwhile or contributing to the betterment of society. The allure of fun is very present in our lives, and with ever increasing technology which makes working less and less of a necessity to prolong society it is becoming an increasing trend.

How is fun a problem? You might ask. Having fun is not. In moderation. Much like substance abuse, the time spent enjoying things could be spent elsewhere.

The moral of You Can't Take It With You applies equally here as well. All the experiences gained in life are lost when the experiencer dies. One can spend a lifetime traveling the world and trying new things but unless those experiences are used to generate something useful to others, postmortem they may as well have not happened. Now, that's not to say that some experiences aren't important.

I went to college to get a Bachelors of Fine Arts degree in Theatre Performance. Ultimately the experience won't matter when I die, but through the experience I gained a greater understanding of what it means to be human and my capacity for compassion and understanding greatly increased. I would not be writing this book had I not gone. In that sense the experience has led to the production of something intended to benefit others and not solely something intended for my pleasure.

Those are experiences worth having.

Having fun is also necessary to relieve stress. Without stress relief people tend to be unproductive and potentially very unstable. It is when fun becomes more important than our relationships or careers that it becomes a detriment. I could spend hours discussing broken relationships that occurred because one partner decided that having fun was more important than the relationship. Such priorities serve only to indulge the hedonistic side of a selfish person and to endanger or destroy a potentially wonderful and worthwhile relationship.

In conclusion, we shouldn't drink or eat in excess, feed our addictions or indulge in a hedonistic lifestyle. It is good to have fun some times, but it isn't good to have fun all the time. It is not wrong to consume in moderation.

Gluttony is not moderation.

Fear

Fear is not listed among "the seven deadly sins". It is included here because it can lead to great harm. It is okay to be afraid. We all have fear. Fear is natural. I'm not saying fear is bad. After all, fear helps keep us alive. If you don't think fear might help you run a little faster from a ravenous lion you are grossly mistaken. However, letting our fears control our actions is not recommended.

Fear can lead us to do things that are harmful to humanity. When people fear marshal law or the apocalypse, they strive to gain excess goods in order to outlast whatever doom may befall them. (See above; Greed). When we fear being alone, we change ourselves (not always for better) to socialize and fit in with others. When we fear the consequences of our actions, we lie and deny accountability. Fear of things we do not understand keeps many people in ignorance (especially with regards to religion). Fear of change prevents us from exploring our humanity and developing new technology. There's a great many things we as people are afraid of, and not everyone is afraid of the same thing.

Fear spawns from a dislike of something, be it material, situational, or even imaginary. Fear also keeps us from treading among wolves so that we are not eaten. It is a primal emotion and preserves us from harm. However, it can also prevent us from doing what is right and good. If a person makes a mistake that results in someone's death, that person might fear the consequences that arise if they are discovered, rather than taking responsibility for what was done. In this way, fear can be destructive to us as a people. Therefore, it is imperative that we understand fear and take great strides to develop courage within ourselves.

Fear is only a sin when it controls our actions and

prevents us from doing what is right. I cannot say that we must learn to not be afraid, because, for one, that is impossible, and for two, fear is healthy. I can't seem to find being eaten by a lion a healthy habit. However, I can say that we should learn to do what is necessary in spite of both rational and irrational fears, because if we cannot the results are disastrous. Fear of black people led to centuries of racism and hatred, and the fear of witches resulted in the deaths of many innocent god fearing people during the Salem witch trials. These are just a few examples and there are many more. Open up a history book and you'll find them in spades.

  Fear is a distressing emotion aroused by impending danger, evil, pain, etc. Whether the threat is real or imagined. (Dictionary.com Fear) With this definition in mind, fear is in many ways a hollow thing. Fear exists before something happens. It has no substance. When we fear it is because we wish to avoid something, be it for ourselves or someone or something else. Its counterpoint is hope, which occurs when we wish for something to occur that has not yet occurred. Both of these come from thinking of the self. Fear and hope are our desire to avoid or realize something. As stated rather simply in the Tao Te Ching: "Hope is as hollow as fear." "Hope and fear are both phantoms that arise from thinking of the self. When we don't see the self as self, what do we have to fear?" (13) Fear and hope are both anticipations of what could be, not necessarily what will be, nor what is or has already been.

  I once knew a woman who shouted and yelled at others who did not agree with her opinions. She was so afraid that people were going to do something awful to her or to others. It did not occur to her that those people had no desire to hurt anyone. Her fear made her believe they would and so she caused a great deal of harm to those she cared about. In a more specific example, she was afraid that her boyfriend was going to become an overbearing husband

and subject her to his will for the rest of her life if they got married. It did not dawn on her that he had no desire to imprison her or subjugate her. He just wanted make her happy. After all, he loved her dearly. Why would he want to hurt her? But that didn't matter. She gave into her fear so completely that on several occasions she accused him of being sexist. She yelled at him, she cried at him, and if she had been a more physically expressive person she probably would have started beating him. This was just one of many fears she possessed but I won't go into further detail. This woman was a prisoner of her own fears because she let those fears dictate her actions. She had great potential to become a wonderful person and treasure her relationships, but in order to accomplish that she needed to learn to be courageous in spite of her fears.

    Another great example of the expression of fear is bigotry. Bigotry sometimes arises not out of pride but out of fear of something we don't understand. In the context of religious bigotry, many people have a difficult time truly understanding the workings of a higher power. To assuage their fear they begin to blindly follow what they've been told without questioning whether it is true or not and ultimately treat others poorly because of it. When fear takes hold sometimes people become bigots and determine that anything contrary to their own belief must therefor be evil. That is one way religious wars arise. When the enemy is considered to be evil it is a lot easier to forget about the enemies' humanity and kill without feeling bad about it. That is the same as not recognizing your fellow man as human.

    So, how can we fight our fears? They are instinctual. They are inherent to our beings. How can we fight against something so core to our being?

    Firstly, and foremost it is necessary for us to control our actions. If we let fear take the wheel and steer we are setting ourselves up for trouble. Like I said, fear is not inherently evil. It is an emotion we were given for a reason. In order for something to be evil it must be selfish, intentional and destructive. Fear arises out of the self since we are the one experiencing our own fear. We are afraid because we are concerned with our safety or the safety of others, or because we suspect that our desires will not be met. Fear itself is not intentional, it is instinctual. So how can it be a sin? It starts to become evil when it drives our action. Actions are intentional. We make a choice to cower or lash out, to fight or run away. When it drives action, fear becomes a vehicle for intention. Finally, fear must be destructive. If action taken (or not taken) due to our fear prevents us from doing the right thing, or causes us to hurt others, it becomes destructive, much like the actions of the girl I mentioned earlier.

In short, we shouldn't let our fears control our actions. We need simply let them inform us of potential dangers. This is why a calm and steady mind is so important.

Apathy

Apathy is also not listed among "the seven deadly sins". It is included here because it too can lead to great harm. Apathy is a lack of interest or concern for something. There are an awful lot of things in this world a person could care about. Not all of them are worthy of concern to be sure. With so many things, how can we determine what we should care about and not care about? The discussion on what things should and should not be of concern could go on endlessly, so instead we will focus on the most important kind of apathy: Shouldn't we care about our fellow human beings?

When we cease to care about the safety and sensitivity of others, we are little better than sociopaths. The lack of concern for others opens up terrible possibilities when combined with other selfish intentions. With regards to Bigotry, apathy toward our fellow man can lead us as far as ethnic cleansing.

Remember Stan? It was his lack of compassion coupled with his pride that caused him to deeply wound a friend. Had he truly been concerned for her, he would never have acted like he did. He would have apologized from the get-go and remembered that she was his friend. None of us want to hurt our friends, for sure. However, when we forget about the feelings of others, even those we love or care for, we wound them and act horribly.

When I was growing up and even now today, I remember hearing people my age saying things like "we should just kill all of the gays" or "Muslims should be shot on sight." I recall many people who firmly believed in the principle "wouldn't it be better if there were no [insert category of people here] in the world". Looking back, I think of all of those people and consider what drove them to think even for a moment that any group of people needed to be shot and killed. The world is filled with people of all kinds of nations, cultures, religions, skin colors, thoughts and beliefs. To remove one of them is to deprive humanity of the growth that diversity brings. Humanity is not just one color or thought, but an evolving society with many things to learn and many questions to discover answers to. Imagine for a moment a world where those selfish thoughts were brought to fruition. Whatever unique perspective a group of people have would be lost, and nothing learned from them. We would all be one color, one thought, one belief, and stuck in our stubborn ways. No growth. We would be no closer to realizing the truth than a pine tree understanding space travel.

Typically when a person ignores the humanity of another, it is because there is some trait, behavior or belief that the person feels is inconvenient. If a person believes that the Mexican population is full of thieves and drug lords, they might feel that the world is better off with all Mexicans for example (not that those kinds of people are limited to Mexico. They can be found all over the world). How is that going to help us solve our problems? Shouldn't we seek a world where we as a society solve the problems of drug sales and theft that we face worldwide? How is committing genocide going to accomplish a better world? Additionally, when one person is killed, the entire family suffers. When millions are killed, the world suffers.

Sometimes we think "wouldn't the world be better if we just got rid of all of the horrible people?" A better question is this: Wouldn't the world be better if we could teach everyone to be tolerant of others, and compassionate toward their fellow human beings? Wouldn't the world be better if we could teach all the horrible people to be wonderful people?

If you think even for a moment that wars aren't fought because people have selfish desires and have become apathetic toward their fellow man, guess again. The crusades began because Europeans wanted wealth and they forgot that their enemies were human beings. The American Civil war was about treating other humans like humans instead of property when you boil right down to it. We've fought those war before. If we're going to avoid it happening again, we have to learn to become empathetic not apathetic.

It's okay not to care about the weather outside, or what sports team won the big cup. There are too many vast and different topics a person could care about than a person can imagine. On a foundational level, at the very least, we should learn to care for the people we share this world with.

Falsehood/Ignorance

Falsehood and ignorance are also not among the seven deadly sins. I've included them as one group because they are both about a lack of truth and knowledge which can be harmful.

Falsehood

When truth is avoided, altered or ignored a falsehood is created. When spoken, this is known as a lie. When thought of, this is known as a misconception or ignorance.

Everyone lies. Why? Early in life we lie to avoid the blame and the punishment that comes along with it. No child likes to be yelled at or beaten. If telling a lie helps us avoid shouting or physical abuse then we are extremely likely to lie. Later in life it becomes a habit. When we are young, our sense of responsibility is not developed and we haven't cultivated the strength necessary to take responsibility for our actions. As we grow older, it becomes easier to tell the truth, to do what we say we will and to show things as they are. One commonality found between most faiths is to live and speak the truth and not tell lies.

Slander and hypocrisy are two specific types of falsehoods that can cause great harm that fall into this category.

Slander is when you make another person or group of people look bad by saying things that aren't true or presenting things in a poor light by leaving facts out of your statements. A slanderer has little regard for their fellow man. There are a lot of reasons people slander each other but the main cause is typically the same. We slander because the result of our slander could lead to an outcome we desire. Slander breeds mistrust. It is hard to trust in others when they are quick to turn around and point out our flaws. Misconceptions also arise out of slander. If John tells us that Joe doesn't like Christians, we might think it true, even if Joe does like Christians. Then we think that Joe is religiously biased. It is hard to see what is truth and what is not when people lie.

Hypocrisy is when you say one thing, such as "people shouldn't fight each other", and then do contrary to what you said, in this case going out and fighting each other. Bare in mind that a hypocrite can be so in different ways. A person who says one thing and does another and then claims to be innocent of all wrongdoing is one type of hypocrite, and in my opinion the worse of the two. The second being a person who says one thing and does another, admits to it and is not proud of their own actions. Though such a one is still a hypocrite, at least they are honest about it. The phrase "do as I say, not as I do" sums up that attitude well. Many people tend to fall into hypocrisy at some point (and hopefully for a very short period of time). We don't need to beat ourselves up over it. We need to simply acknowledge our hypocrisy and take responsibility for our actions. Then we can try to change ourselves.

    Sometimes we lie to make ourselves look more intelligent (ah, the joys of selfish pride). This classic art is known colloquially as "a load of bull". I have seen it practiced on the grandest of stages in the political world of the United States of America. The result was the ignorance of a large portion of an entire nation. So why do we lie to make ourselves look better? Pride maybe? Shame, perhaps? Sometimes we lie to avoid pain. It's hard sometimes to tell the truth, especially when the truth is that we made a mistake. Nobody likes to be known for their mistakes. We spend an awful lot of time pointing them out to each other, who can blame us? Nobody likes that kind of negativity. However, if everyone told the truth and everyone forgave each other for their mistakes, maybe we would be more inclined to tell the truth in the first place. As children we lie to avoid punishment. If there were no punishment, but merely a modification of behaviors through conditioning and positive reinforcement, perhaps we would not lie as children and grown into more honest adults.

There is a Hindu/Indian saying: Speak what is pleasant, speak what is true, but never speak an unpleasant truth. This saying is a good philosophy, but it is incomplete. The reason I feel this statement to be incomplete is this: You should not speak an unpleasant truth perhaps, but there are times when you must speak the unpleasant truth to stave off the destruction that would be caused by ignorance.

Now let's take a look at an example of dishonesty that could be very controversial. Let us say that you are hiding a family of Jews in the attic of your house. Now let us say that Nazi soldiers stop by looking for Jewish people so that they can be rounded up and killed. They ask you if there are any Jews in your home. Do you tell them? Or do you lie? How do we decide when it is okay to lie and when it is not okay? In this example, truly, it is the fault of the soldiers that wish to kill the Jews for acting in a way which might force us to lie about whether or not we are harboring Jewish people. Most people would agree that in this sort of situation the right thing to do is to lie. So where do we draw that line? Dishonesty is bad when it is selfish, destructive and intentional. We should present the truth as often as possible so that, as a society, we can function well and operate on the principles of truth.

Ignorance

When we lead others to believe things that are not true, we create ignorance.
There are many different things people are ignorant about. Of them, one of the greatest places to find ignorance is faith. When we believe something that is not based on truth, it is known as a superstition. Superstitions are usually quite harmless, but they certainly don't allow us to grasp reality. Many major religions have superstitions built into their beliefs or the culture that surrounds them. I won't go

into detail pointing them out because for one they are too numerous to list, and for two some of those beliefs are held dear by many people, perhaps even you. Since the point of this book is not to offend but rather to open minds, I would encourage you to delve into your own beliefs and think about which of them may very well be superstition and which ones are based on truth, and I will leave it at that.

Instead, let's take a look at a superstition that resulted in the loss of many innocent lives. The Salem witch trials were a series of hearings and prosecutions of people accused of witchcraft in colonial Massachusetts between February 1692 and May 1693. All told, twenty people were executed. Why? Because of beliefs based not on fact but superstition. In these trials, men and women were accused of being witches. None of them were. However, a strong overriding belief in witchcraft as well as the fears and selfishness of others led these people to separate from their own kind people they believed were witches. These "witches" were sentenced to death.

If you'd like a great literary example of what these trials were like, I would encourage you to read The Crucible by Arthur Miller. In his story, you see how a young woman preys on the superstitions of the townsfolk in order to coerce a grown man to sleep with her. It doesn't end well for him or a majority of the townsfolk.

The other kind of ignorance is lack of knowledge. A simple truth: There are a great many things we humans just don't know. Sometimes we theorize using scientific knowledge or past experiences, and sometimes we just make things up that fit but aren't at all true. If the rain comes after a tribal dance and prayer to the rain gods, that doesn't mean the dance and prayer brought the rain. We've proven that scientifically. That is the nature of superstition. If you recall, correlation does not mean causation. The average global temperature has not risen due to the decrease in pirates.

Sometimes we simply don't know the truth. It is okay to lack knowledge of something. None of us are omniscient. However, we should pursue the truth. If I hadn't pursued the truth, I would not be writing this book. If more people would pursue spiritual truths, we would have fewer superstitions and less religious intolerance.

Ignorance is only a sin when it leads to destruction. It is hard to call ignorance intentional, however. Ignorance becomes intentional when we do not take action to dispel ignorance. We often close an eye and move on with our lives because it is just easier that way. It is much simpler to call something an act of God and be done with it than it is to delve deeply into what occurred and why it occurred. That is how a large portion of a nation can feel that the Muslim religion is full of terrorists and violent people in spite of the fact that the religion is by nature a tolerant and understanding one. I won't go into further detail on the American contention with "Muslim" terrorists. The point is that when we don't know everything about something we can either take action to gain understanding and grow as a people, or we can ignore it, brush it off because it is easier to do so and live in ignorance and that ignorance can be very harmful.

Illusions

The last piece of ignorance is subtle but important all the same. This is the influence and distraction of illusions or vain imaginings. Illusions are appearances without substance. People tend to become distracted with the superficial qualities of things and give them great importance, though the substance of those things is little or none. People become concerned more so with how things look and taste and feel than with the content of such things. Perhaps you know someone who is wrapped up with their hair color and what their car looks like. Maybe you know someone who is overly concerned not with who they are in a relationship with but with what their partner looks like and how their relationship appears to others. This is a hollow perception of reality. When a person becomes more concerned with their partner looking beautiful or hansom and going on wild and crazy adventures and all their minutes are filled with romantic notions, the relationship is shallow. It is built on appearance and experiences, not on compassion and unity. When a person spends all their time focusing on the superficial aspects of their life or their self, there is no time to create a meaningful life or develop into a worthwhile person.

Illusions are addictive and enticing. Everyone enjoys a little romance now and again. When we spend our time chasing vanity or the superficial things in this world we open ourselves up to the atrophy of our spirit. We stop caring for what really makes us wholly good and focus instead on what makes us look good. A rotten apple, wrapped in a perfect red skin, is still rotten. When we become weak due to our desire for appearances and unimportant things, we are more likely to give in to selfish desires. Illusions feel nice and thus they serve the self. We have a choice to merely pursue those superficial things or to dig deeper and grow more as a person, therefore the indulgence in illusions is intentional. If we do, we do not spend our time growing into better people. If anything, we tend to fall backwards toward selfish desires. That is when illusion becomes destructive.

Illusions are a distraction from what is real, and in that sense make us ignorant to reality by concerning ourselves only with the surface. When we wrap ourselves up in fiction we lose our grip on reality, but it is okay to have a little romance here and there.

To sum up Falsehood/Ignorance: Truth is. Lies are

not. To progress as a people we need to understand what is true instead of creating things that are not.

Conclusion

    Evil is a selfish intentional act that causes destruction to ourselves, others and the world around us. We can categorize evil actions based on their differences. However, there are common traits that each category shares and all of these revolve around the self.

    The greatest of evils is no specific one of these categories, nor is it a combination of them. The greatest evil we can do is intentionally convince others to do them. Loathsome is the man who sins but worse still is the man who drives others to sin.

"The question is not as to the aggregate amount of suffering inflicted, but as to the moral character of the acts by which the suffering is inflicted." We see this most clearly, when we shift our view from the act itself to its remoter consequences. The hapless animal suffers, dies, "and there is an end": but the man whose sympathies have been deadened, and whose selfishness has been fostered, by the contemplation of pain deliberately inflicted, may be the parent of others equally brutalized, and so bequeath a curse to the future ages. And even if we limit our view to the present time, who can doubt that the degradation of a soul is a greater evil than the suffering of bodily frame? (Carroll 1075)

    As a culture we cannot thrive if we continually try to corrupt one another. One of the ways we corrupt one another is when we attempt to disprove the beliefs of others with disrespect and intolerance. Disproving a belief in this way is destructive, not productive. To do so to others and succeed is to create instability and weakness in our fellow man. Humanity is a collection of people. The weaker the pieces of humanity, the weaker the whole. Of course, there are beliefs that do not follow truth. We should strive to erase such beliefs from ourselves through careful contemplation. That is the nature of self-improvement. If we try to erase the beliefs of others we can cause great harm. How can a person follow good courses of action if they have no foundation to build sound morals upon? To intentionally try to remove those foundational blocks for any reason is to unravel a person because we humans hold on tightly to our beliefs. The result is a lack of faith and unsteady footings. We must promote good will and be constructive in our search for faith if humanity is to thrive.

    Most of the time, our actions aren't driven by a specific desire, but rather a combination of desires. Often times it is difficult to single out one intention when considering the actions of an individual. Sometimes it's truly impossible. Who is to say they truly understand the inner workings of another, let alone understand why they make their own choices? However, if we are trying to determine whether our actions align on the right path or not, we must consider this: The commonality between all sinful acts is the presence of selfish desire, intention and the destructive consequences of those actions. Did it hurt someone or destroy something? Did we do it on purpose? Was it for our own desires or was it selfless? Even if we feel that we are perfect, my hope is that we will at least consider what we do or have done with these things in mind. Without the insight into our own actions we are hopelessly bound to leave hurt and ruin in our wake.

    If we do not understand the truth, what is right or wrong, and why those things are right or wrong, then we do not have a foundation on which to stand against intolerant beliefs.

"If you know the enemy and know yourself, you need not fear the result of a hundred battles. If you know yourself but not the enemy, for every victory gained you will also suffer a defeat. If you know neither the enemy nor yourself, you will succumb in every battle." (Sun Tzu 15)

Altruism

Naturally, if we're going to talk about evil (it is hard not to within the discussion of religious/spiritual behavior) we must also talk about the nature of good. As we discuss good things we should keep in mind how it relates to bigotry. Remember, bigotry is the complete intolerance of differing views and behaviors. Being such, it lacks respect for mankind's progress be it spiritual, moral or ethical. So, how does goodness factor into our discussion for the argument against bigotry? One thing that occurs within the bigoted mind is the dehumanization of our fellow men. One of the reasons this occurs is because we don't recognize the good in others, especially the good intents that others use as a basis for their actions. If we can learn to recognize the good in others we can identify ourselves with others. If we can identify with others, we are more likely to be respectful and tolerant of others and their beliefs. So, let us get to work identifying the good in others.

To start with, if we're going to get into the age old practice of dualistic thinking (good vs evil), we have to understand what sorts of things most people think of as good. The classic word that flows from the mouth almost immediately as an example of good is the word virtue. By definition, a virtue is something humanity likes.

Virtue: A good or admirable quality or potency. (Dictionary.com Virtue)

By this definition, a virtue is not the opposite of the

evil acts I have discussed above. Sin is an act. A virtue is a quality. When I looked to find the things we consider to be virtues, I found a list as long as my arm and many were hardly virtues at all. Here is the list I came up with. You'll notice some contradictions within it as well as qualities that do not protect us from evil but are still admirable to some degree.

Acceptance, ambition, assertiveness, attention, autonomy, awareness, balance, benevolence, candor, cautiousness, charisma, charity, chastity, chivalry, citizenship, cleanliness, commitment, compassion, confidence, conscientiousness, consideration, contentment, continence, cooperativeness, courage, courteousness, creativity, curiosity, dependability, detachment, determination, diligence, discernment, endurance, equanimity, fairness, faithfulness, fidelity, freedom, friendliness, flexibility, foresight (psychology), forgiveness, frugality, generosity, gentleness, goodness, good temper, gratitude, helpfulness, honesty, honor, happiness, hospitality, humility, humor, impartiality, independence, industry, integrity, intuition, inventiveness, justice, kindness, knowledge, logic, loyalty, meekness, mercy, mindfulness, moderation, modesty, morality, nonviolence, obedience, openness, order, patience, peacefulness, perseverance, philomathy, piety, potential, prudence, purity, reason, readiness, remembrance, resilience, respectfulness, responsibility, restraint, self-reliance, self-respect, sensitivity, service, sharing, sincerity, silence, solidarity, spirituality, sportsmanship, stability, subsidiarity, tactfulness, temperance, tenacity, thoughtfulness, trustworthiness, tolerance, understanding, unity, unpretentiousness, vigilance, wealth, wisdom.

Some of these virtues are simply states of being or qualities that in some instances are beneficial and in others detrimental. Some of the things listed are acts. Some are simply states of being. Some are good in some instances and bad in others. Some are inherent and some acquirable. We should note that a virtue is defined as either good or admirable. Some people admire terrible things in others. For example, ruthlessness, dominance and shamelessness. Perhaps there are times when such qualities are good, but those qualities are not always a good thing. Humanity doesn't care much for the tyrant though the tyrant may be admired for such virtues. Therefore a virtue is not the antithesis of evil. So what is?

As mentioned before, sin is an act. So too must its opposite be an act. We have choices to make in life and those choices are sometimes between doing the right thing or doing the wrong thing. If you look in the dictionary for an antonym to sin, you'll find the words goodness, behavior and morality. We are looking for a type of behavior that is a goodness.

Morality is a peculiar term as it is defined as conformity to the rules of right conduct; moral or virtuous conduct. (Dictionary.com Morality)

Now there's that word virtue again. So let's look at the word "moral" for a moment.

A moral is a principle or rule of right conduct. "Right conduct" is a potentially subjective term when looked at in a social context. Of course, when looked at with spiritual context it refers to "God's laws" and goodness, surely. In a social context, if a society feels that a behavior is right, then the behavior is moral. There are many acceptable behaviors within a society that are certainly not acceptable in many religions, such as sexual conduct, the death sentence, retribution and drug use. In this sense, moral is a subjective term. When you look at a moral within a spiritual context, morality is not subjective but universal, as it applies to all of mankind, not just a particular society.

So, is a moral the opposite of sin? Sin is an act. A moral is a rule or principle. Rules are typically a "do this" or "don't do that" or "when this, that". A moral is a rule that influences action but is not the action itself. Remember, we are trying to recognize the good works in others. A rule is something a person follows, not an action.

If what we are searching for isn't morals (rules) and it isn't virtues (qualities), then what is it we must search for in others? The answer is altruism. An altruism is the principle or practice of unselfish concern for, or the devotion to, the welfare of others. The term "principle" is present such as it would be in morals but I will be referring to altruism as a practice and therefore action.

Both good and evil are the result of choice. After all, evil is an intentional act that is selfish and destructive. Good must then be an intentional act that is selfless and nurturing to ourselves, others and the world around us. There are many acts that are admirable but we are going to focus on those acts that are antithesis to those things which we consider to be evil, for those acts are the ones that help humanity to live in peace and thrive as a society by means of eliminating suffering.

"In the Old Testament, no doubt, rewards and punishments are constantly appealed to as motives for action. That teaching is best for children, and the Israelites seem to have been, mentally, utter children. We guide our children thus, at first: but we appeal, as soon as possible, to their innate sense of Right and Wrong: and, when that stage is safely past, we appeal to the highest motive of all, the desire for likeness to, and union with, the Supreme Good."
(Lewis Carroll 396)

Virtues

How can we perform selfless acts? Surely, when you analyze every decision you've ever made you made it because it is what your self wanted, either because you desired the outcome or because you wished to avoid the alternatives. We always act out of the self. It is impossible not to. Our bodies perform the acts based on the will. So how can we perform a truly selfless act? The answer is simple: We can't. Try as you might, all that you do you do because you choose to based on some desire you possess. However, there is a way to perform good deeds, which at a glance does seem selfless. When a person helps someone else or does a great deed, often it fills them with positive feelings. It feels great to help someone in need, or to bring a smile to someone in despair. When we take action in order to help others, we do it because it is satisfying. We do it because it makes us feel good about what we do. This is the essence of acting selflessly. You will always choose to do what you want but if what you want is to help others, then your selfishness has surpassed the self and affects the world around you.

Virtues are not the opposite of evil. A virtue is a frame of mind and a strength of the soul. A virtue can lessen the tendency to perform intentional selfish acts of destruction. Destroying destruction in a sense. A virtue is also the tendency to perform selfless acts and acts that benefit humanity. A virtue is an improvement of the self. The list of virtues is incredibly long and probably could not be summed up with what I came up with in this writing. So, I will focus more on categories of altruism rather than virtues. Unlike evil acts which arise from selfish desires, altruistic behaviors are practiced skills that enable us to resist our urges and be productive with ourselves. Virtues, which are traits, encourage altruistic behavior which is opposite selfish, intentional, destructive acts.

Altruism is the principle or practice of unselfish concern for or devotion to the welfare of others.

(Dictionary.com Altruism) The acts that nurture our society and our world derive from a concern for others as well as the devotion to improving the self. (Note that it is not devotion to the self.) Altruism is the path to becoming a better us and a person truly worth being. Altruistic behavior consists primarily of self-control, charity, courage, industry, honesty, empathy and good will.

- Self-control: The act of resisting, or not acting on, impulse or instinct, such as moderation or abstention. (the avoidance of greed, gluttony, wrath and lust) abstention, chastity, moderation, calmness. Without self-control we tend to act selfishly.

- Charity: The act of giving to others who will truly grow and benefit from what is given. (opposite greed) charitable in argument, non-judgment, humbleness, donation

- Courage: The act of doing the right thing in the presence of fear. (opposite fear, opposite jealousy)

- Industry: The practice of making use of your time on this earth. (opposite sloth and ignorance)

- Honesty: The practice of speaking and including truth and acting truthfully. (Opposite falsehood)

- Empathy: The psychological identification with or vicarious experience of the feelings, thoughts or attitudes of another. (Dictionary.com Empathy) (Opposite apathy and pride) community, compassion, mercy, humbleness

- Good Will: the desire for others to have good things and desirable circumstances. (Opposite envy)

Self Control

This is a very large category because there are many ways in which a person can control themselves. A person can control their thoughts and actions which in turn control and influence bodily health, create a stable and strong mind, and develop the ability to resist temptation and excess in spite of personal desires. While we won't go into complete detail on all the ways a person can exercise self control, we will talk about how self control helps us to avoid greed, gluttony, wrath and lust by means of abstention, chastity, moderation and calmness.

Of all the altruisms and virtues one might embody and possess, the greatest of these is self control. Without control of the self, how can you intentionally perform selfless acts? We always act out of the self, remember? If we aren't in control of our own selves then we are not in control of our actions and thus we give in to weakness and desire. (Upanishads Vol 2 10)

Bodily Health

There is a Chinese saying that goes something like this: "Long of limb, long of sinew, long of life."

Bodily health is potentially a cure for the effects of sloth. Energy begets energy. The more you do, the more you are capable of doing. There have been a great many studies about the chemical balances within the body both in healthy and unhealthy people. The simple truth is this: A healthy person is more capable of rational thought and balanced emotions. Without bodily health, concentration and steadiness of the mind becomes more and more difficult. Without proper health, a person becomes depressed, anxious, irrational and any number of other mental imbalances. (Physical and Mental Health)

I once knew a woman whose chemical imbalance became severe. She began to hallucinate. She said horrible things to her husband and claimed she had cheated on him and did everything she could to push him away. She lashed out at everyone and was in complete despair. She was quickly committed to a mental institution. While this is an extreme case, it shows how poor health can result in destructive action. Once she was restored to a proper mental state she apologized for her behavior to everyone she had been in contact with. Simply put, she wasn't herself.

If you want to try a simple experiment to see if this is true, go out and exercise. Work out for a half an hour and exhaust yourself. Do this every three days and you will find that you have more energy and generally a better disposition. With a better disposition, you will be more relaxed and able to make decisions based on proper thinking, rather than on stress, depression and anxiety. Of all the virtues one might possess, this is the most external. However, it will make a great impact on the ease of embodying other altruistic behavior and acting rationally.

In reading the Upanishads, you will find a great deal of stress placed upon the vital breath. It is the most important organ. The other organs are also important, but the breath is the greatest. When our health is poor, so too our breathing. When we run and exercise, our lung capacity increases and allows our body to function better.

Keep the body in good shape and you will live longer and be a more balanced person.

Concentration and Steadiness of Mind

Have you ever been so upset/afraid/nervous/in love that you were unable to think clearly? Concentration is a great skill yet it is difficult to develop when we give in to our emotions and desires. Without proper concentration and a steady mind, we tend to become impatient and make rash decisions. The greatest fighters keep a calm mind on the battlefield, the greatest of debates involve those who can think clearly. A clear and steady mind is an incredible asset to those wishing to live a good life without making quite so many bad decisions.

Concentration is the ability to focus our minds on the object at hand. A steady mind allows concentration during stressful situations.

Sometimes when we are in love we become consumed with emotion. In those situations we may allow those we love to do terrible things and we brush it off since our loved one is important to us. Worse yet, we might do things we shouldn't in the name of our love. For example, if our loved one is a relentless alcoholic, we might not be willing to acknowledge that there is a problem. We may even join them if we greatly desire their company.

When we are exceedingly fearful, we are incapable of thinking clearly. The "Fight or flight" instinct is an instinct intended to keep us alive. However, sometimes the fight or flight response appears in places where we are not at risk of death or physical injury, such as within social encounters. People tend to become defensive when they feel socially threatened. Without a calm and steady mind the results tend to be either aggression or withdrawal.

A steady mind is the only cure for panic. Panic is defined as a sudden overwhelming fear, with or without cause that produces hysterical or irrational behavior and often spreads quickly through a group of persons or animals.(Dictionary.com Panic) Scary, isn't it? Irrational behavior occurs in a variety of situations, anywhere from a cheating wife or husband, or not getting the job we desperately needed. Have you ever acted irrationally in response to adverse situations and then later, after reflecting on what happened, see clearly and easily what the better action would have been? Perhaps, had you maintained a steady mind and concentrated on the problem at hand, you wouldn't have run for the nearest exit, but rather had the strength to do the right thing. Courage is necessary to do things in spite of our fears. A steady mind allows us to be courageous.

Have you ever met someone you would classify as a "jar-head"? That is to say, someone who has spent little to no time at all developing their mind. Just like our bodies, when we do not exercise our minds, we get sick. An unhealthy mind is irrational and does not think clearly. Those without good mental capacity can make very poor decisions. How can you decide between a good action and a bad one when you can't differentiate between the two? That is one of the reasons the development of faith is so important. When you can easily tell what is right and what is wrong, you can make the best decisions. When you don't develop the mind how can you make that distinction?

A proper faith requires us to use and develop our intelligence. After all, it is the mind that perceives and interprets the truth. The body only collects data. It is the mind that receives and processes the data.

During the 1600's several European scientists, including Galileo and Kepler, developed mathematical models and telescopic observations to prove that the earth circled the sun in a predictable manner, contrary to the teachings of the Catholic Church which assumed that the earth was at the center of the universe with the sun, moon and planets circling it. Galileo, in particular, followed the dictates of his mind over the religious teachings of the times to persist in the promotion of this new idea, ultimately choosing house arrest by the church, rather than to denounce his own ideas. To say the least, it was a stressful time. However, he kept his mind steady and was thus able to act appropriately to serve a greater purpose. The same thing applies to our development today. To dispel ignorance, we must develop the mind in order to observe the truth. Without our minds, we are merely animals acting on instinct. To surpass our fight or flight response, we must maintain a steady mind. Without a steady mind, we are agents of panic and chaos.

Moderation

      Everything in moderation. You have possibly heard that phrase at least once in your lifetime. Why is it so difficult for us to live to this principle? If you've ever eaten too much candy or slept for far too long, you know all to well what exceeding moderation can do to a person. It makes us sick. This is true in terms of diet and exercise, but also in spirit. When you spend all of your time exercising, you don't spend any of your time in thought. When you spend all of your time in thought, you spend none of it in exercise. If you devote all of your time to religion, where then is your time for friends and family?
      Moderation is restraint or avoidance of extremes or excess. That means avoiding both ends of the spectrum. For example, a person can moderate their intake of religious observance, as well as the absence thereof. A person can live and relish in social situations sometimes and avoid those situations at other times. When we moderate our behavior we are mitigating the immersion in or absence of a particular thing.
      So how does moderation help us deal with our destructive, selfish and deliberate acts? There are two ways in which moderation allows us to thrive and mitigate poor choices. The first of which is fairly obvious. Mankind is an imperfect species. We possess strong intellect but we often succumb to our desires. By practicing moderation, we succumb to our desires less frequently. The simple truth is this: many of us are incapable of resisting our desires one hundred percent of the time. If we can't stop ourselves from giving in to our desires completely, isn't it better to at least

resist them sometimes instead of always giving in to them? That's not to say that we should allow ourselves to give in when we can just as easily resist. It is merely to encourage the practice of abstaining from an act so that when it really truly matters most we are at least capable of resisting our desires so as not to act selfishly to the detriment of ourselves, others, or the world around us. In short, practice makes perfect. The more you practice, the easier things become. This is true in sports, in art, in fighting addictions, in being a better person, in almost anything. If we practice moderation we will be able to control ourselves more easily when it really matters.

    The second benefit of moderation is not so obvious. It is intelligence. As strange as it may sound, moderation can actually teach you more than you would learn by otherwise overindulging. When you moderate your actions, you open yourself up to discovering the benefits of that action's absence as well as its presence. Let's look at this with regards to spiritual development for a moment. Imagine, for a moment, that a person is completely and absolutely consumed by the practice of attending church and reciting verses from a holy book of some kind. This sort of extreme may result in a kind of spiritual ignorance. How can a person discover truth if they refuse to seek it? Reciting rhetoric ad nauseum does not increase intelligence, after all. It just deepens the thing being repeated in our mind until we can see little else beside it. Imagine now, on the other hand, the same person forgoes any spiritual development at all, doesn't go to church, doesn't seek truth, simply stays at home and watches television. This also results in ignorance. Now let's say that this person spends a day each week in spiritual devotion to his/her religion, and the rest of the time experiencing the world. This moderation of spiritual observance allows the person to see the nature of the world, and with it gain some sense of truth, and at the same time practice faith, develop a strength of spiritual belief and hopefully a strong moral compass that goes along with it. In this example, moderation has removed the tendency toward ignorance by keeping the person away from extremes.

Too much of any one thing is not healthy for the human spirit. Too much food is gluttony and makes us fat, too little makes us starve. An excess of lust makes us slaves to our desires, a lack thereof prevents procreation and the continuation of our genes. An excess of wrath is the purest form of destruction but a lack of anger makes us complacent to harmful circumstances. If we are solely greedy we have nothing but our money and if overly generous we have nothing to keep ourselves alive.

Self control is the only means by which we can resist desires, strengthen and grow as a people, and perform selfless acts even when it is difficult to do so. We gain self control by taking care of our bodies, developing our minds and moderating the fulfillment of our desires.

"No spiritual progress is possible without purity of heart. The attainment of this purity is a gradual process. Common people of dull intellect disobey the scriptures and act whimsically, impelled by their natural impulses, and reap disastrous results. But if the enjoyment of these desires is controlled by certain Vedic rituals, they are gradually sublimated." (Upanishads Vol. 4 94)

Charity

Being charitable means to be generous in donations or gifts to relieve the needs of the indigent, ill or helpless. (Dictionary.com Charitable) Being charitable does not mean simply giving things to others. You can donate all day long to a person or cause and it would not be charity.

Charity can only be given to those who truly need it. So how can we be charitable?

Charity should be like the breath. If we do not inhale, we cannot exhale. If we do not exhale we cannot inhale. If all we do is give to others more than is necessary, our selves will fall to ruin because we are not taken care of. If we are in ruin we cannot give to others because we lack the means to do so. Everyone struggles when nobody gives. Everyone struggles when everyone takes. If we only take care of ourselves and do not give to others when it is necessary, they will struggle as well and will see no reason to take care of us when we are desperate. Additionally, if we give to those who do not need it, we enable them to become lazy and weak. When we leave those we gave to needlessly, the crutch we have provided disappears and all they have to stand on is their own laziness and weakness. That kind of generosity leads to ruin. Charity where it is not needed leads to a lazy society and weak individuals. Charity is an ebb and flow, and you should give what you can afford where it is needed, but you should not give needlessly to those who do not truly need it.

Beggars are a frustrating people. Often, those who beg are not those who really need help. Think for a moment about how much time a beggar spends begging for money on the street. If the same amount of time was spent contributing to society in the form of work that same beggar could be making decent money and providing a sound benefit to society. Typically speaking, those who truly need help are striving desperately with every breath just to make it by. They are too prideful to ask for help, and often we turn a blind eye to their need. To be charitable, we need to keep our eyes open for those who are in need and help them out as best we can until they can stand on their own. With many beggars, on the other hand, we have a people who have learned that they can survive without working. To give to a beggar enables the behavior and allows parts of our society to become lazy. The solution to this kind of ruinous generosity is simply to not give to those who beg. Sounds harsh, doesn't it?

Charity, when done properly, can make a great impact on a person's life and once the impact has been made the charity can move forward. I once had a friend who was living in dire straights. He was living in a friend's home without proper flooring or a window. The room was scarcely large enough to accommodate him and he had little more than a mattress to sleep on. He had been unemployed for years and had no success trying to find work to earn his living. He had no transportation to get to a job and even if he did, he was near sighted so he couldn't properly drive to work legally without risking an accident. The family he was living with told him he had to pay rent or move out, and without a job there was only one possible outcome. Out of disgust for the way he was living, I offered to help him out. I brought him into my home until we could get him a job. Once that had been done, we worked toward getting him a proper pair of glasses. He saved up to purchase a vehicle and eventually got one. The windshield was cracked and needed replaced, however. I insisted that I buy him his new windshield since he couldn't afford it. It took him a minute to swallow his pride, but now he is able to stand on his own. He has a full time job, his own apartment and is getting by just fine. If I hadn't stepped in when I did it would have been a matter of time before he became homeless. I did what I did because it was needed. I used my anger at his living arrangements to drive me to help him and I gave him what he needed most. He never asked for it, he never begged. Someday, I believe he'll pay it forward, which will be of great benefit to someone else.

We can be charitable to one another with more than just wealth and goods. Another form of charity is in giving others the benefit of the doubt. We can be charitable in argumentation. Being charitable in this sense is acknowledging the perspective of others even though we may believe them to be wrong. For all we know, we are wrong in our own perspective or are missing a crucial piece of the puzzle. So we must be charitable if we are to recognize truth. In this sense we are charitable by being generous in allowing others to speak and exercise their opinions and beliefs because they need to be able to express those beliefs. When we don't listen to or consider the beliefs of others we are poor in understanding. By being charitable in argumentation can better reach an understanding of each other, recognize our own flaws and shortcomings, and as a community be more likely to reach the truth.

Being charitable in argument is a virtue a bigot does not possess.

Charity is like the breath. When we inhale, we insure that we are kept healthy and well, when we exhale we benefit others, and that breath allows for the greatest benefit for mankind. If we can learn to be charitable in thought and action, mankind cannot help but to become wealthy beyond measure.

Courage

In order to be courageous, we must also be afraid. Courage is not the absence of fear, but the choice to act in spite of our fear. Fear keeps us alive. Courage makes us strong. By definition, courage is a virtue. Courage becomes altruistic when it allows us to do what is right and do what is necessary. It can be something as small as standing up for ourselves, or as large as facing down a lion without a weapon to defend ourselves. Who is to say which is the greatest example of courage?

Courage is like a muscle. The more you exercise it, the stronger it becomes. The less you use it, the weaker. I once worked with a man who was overbearing, aggressive and stubborn. He was not someone I wanted to deal with. I feared encounters with this person because I had learned that he would use every opportunity to tell me what to do and how to do it without considering my own stances on policies and procedures and he possessed the influence to potentially end my career. I knew that avoiding him forever was not going to happen short of losing my job, but I was so out of practice in dealing with such an overbearing man that it took great labors to convince myself to tough it out. In short, my courage had atrophied. So I began to intentionally force myself into encounters with that man within the course of my job. Dealing with him was no easier, and surely he was still a threat to my professional career. However, the more I took in a deep breath and dove into the waters to deal with him, the more I was capable of having those encounters with him. Was this kind of courage truly amazing? Probably not. However, I was afraid to deal with him and chose to do so in spite of my fear. That is the essence of courage.

Most other species on our planet live in harmony with others of the same species. They have a community built on trust. So why don't we? It is truly puzzling. Why should we fear each other? Rather, if there is a person whom we fear, shouldn't we learn to understand them? Through understanding, fear dissipates. Often times we are afraid of others because we do not know what that person is going to do. Fear of the unknown is incredibly common.

When it becomes a habit to face our fears we are capable of doing the most good. Fear, as described before, is an aversion to possibilities. We fear what might happen, not what is happening. When we accept the possibility of things we fear, understand why we fear them and how to deal with the outcomes of what we fear, we stop fearing and become all the more capable of dealing with those situations objectively. If what we value most is our own life, we have given in to selfishness. If fear governs our actions, we will tend to act according to those fears. Fear can lead us to take actions that go against our moral grains. Courage allows us to do what is right in the face of what is truly terrifying.

In my youth I was exposed to severe heights. I became irrationally afraid of high places up until my sophomore year in college. I was so afraid of falling and the potential injury that might follow in spite of the fact that I had never actually fallen. My fear was so severe that I became paralyzed by them and unable to act when confronted with situations involving heights. Fear had taken hold of my actions and I knew it. To confront my fears in my sophomore year in college I volunteered to work in the catwalks of a theater knowing full well that I was terrified of heights. I had forced myself into a situation where I would have to confront my fear. And I did. I slowly grew accustomed to it and began to understand what factors would contribute to a fall and what actions would prevent it. I had to learn to trust my body to do what I told it to and by the end of the year I was capable of dangling off the edge of the catwalks by just my feet and a secure harness, leaning my full torso out over a thirty foot drop. I had conquered my fear. Through that experience I learned that with understanding and self-control I was able to successfully fight my fear.

Now, when I run across people who are paralyzed by their fear of heights, I encourage them to face their fear and to take actions within a reasonably safe environment. The results are astounding. Those people who were before terrified of climbing up a ten foot ladder now do it with ease. They admit that there is still fear there, but they possess the courage to accomplish tasks in spite of their fear.

Courage is the only way to fight the evils of fear. It is the only medicine for jealous fear. While trust helps remove jealousy, courage is necessary for the establishment of trust. It takes courage to place your welfare in the hands of others. If you can be courageous, fear will not determine your actions.

Industry

Industry is an energetic devotion to productive activity. I could speak to the advancement of human technology and research, but the greater concern in this context is with the habit of productive activity. Humanity always strives to advance, for better or for worse, and that advancement may be to the benefit or detriment of society. In that sense, industry is not altruistic. It is simply movement forward as opposed to regression.

As an altruistic behavior, industry is the process of acting instead of doing nothing and doing something productive instead of something pointless. The simplest form of industry is physical exercise. Recognizing that exercise is truly of benefit to the person exercising (as described in self-control), as a process it requires time and energy. Its productivity or purpose is that of building a stronger body. It takes dedication to perform regular exercise. In a more complex example, let's look at the painter. The painter has to gather supplies, practice the art, take the time to perform and perfect their skill to produce something that is nice to look at or profound in its concept. Without industry, the canvas is blank, the supplies are insufficient and the skill of the artist is poorly developed. Another example is that of the blacksmith. A blacksmith performs tiring labor lifting metal, heating and tending the furnace, hammering away at the piece, all to create a tool for the benefit of mankind. It isn't easy and it requires great practice, patience and the development of skill. Without the blacksmith it would have been impossible to advance human technology to the point we have reached today by the process of forming metal into desirable shapes we can use as tools. If a blacksmith is not industrious, a low quantity of poor quality metal tools are the result and the benefit to mankind is significantly reduced. Furthermore, the blacksmith has not improved in skill and does not realize the benefit his skill might have had for his fellow man. We would never have surpassed the iron age if it weren't for industrious blacksmiths.

Industry (the commitment to action) is the only guard against sloth. It takes self-control to devote oneself to performing tiring actions. Work is hard. The tendency for some people is to do as little as possible for the greatest gain. This minimalistic trend in our nature simply encourages us to be lazy and through our laziness we atrophy. It took incredible efforts of industry to survive the creatures of the wild, to endure the harshness of our environment and to advance our knowledge and technology as a species over the course of millennia. These days, especially here in America, people just want to laze around watching television and enjoy things rather than strive to improve themselves and develop worthwhile endeavors for the sake of their fellow man. We expect to have some sort of easy job that pays tons of money so we don't have to work hard for the things we want. Does that help us to grow stronger or develop a strong society? Or is the strength of our society weakening because of it? Without industry, we atrophy. There is no permanent state of strength. A colleague of mine said it best. Every moment we aren't practicing or working we are getting worse. That's not to say that we can't have time to rest to repair ourselves, but like a bird in flight, if we aren't flapping our wings then we are succumbing to gravity.

The desire to be industrious is a virtue because it is a quality. To practice industry is altruistic. It is practice that keeps us strong. Industry is something we must choose to do that benefits ourselves and others and is necessary to prevent our own atrophy.

Honesty

Honesty really is the best policy, isn't it? We've already talked a lot about falsehood and how it misleads others, so let's talk about its antithesis. Honesty is truthfulness, sincerity and frankness. (Dictionary.com Honesty) That is, expressing what is true and not what is false. However, honesty is not limited to our words. We can act in ways that deceive just as easily as we can speak what is not true. For example (and perhaps in an amusing one) a person might get dressed in exercise clothing to make it seem like they work out or go to the gym when in truth that person does not, so as to create a false impression of themselves. A sad fact of our society is that there are people who engage in deceitful behavior to better their position in society or gain favor or influence with their friends.

Honesty is hardest when the truth shows our mistakes and flaws and makes us responsible for things we shouldn't have done. We learn this habit from a very young age. Often, the first lie we tell is to prevent ourselves from getting in trouble with our parents when we've done something we shouldn't have. It's the old "hand in the cookie jar" scenario. We might blame our siblings or insist that it wasn't us when we've broken the rules because we fear the punishment for doing something wrong. This kind of dishonesty is completely self-serving and begins the habit of telling lies to avoid punishment. Where does this behavior come from? Parents often punish children for breaking the rules. We aren't typically rewarded for taking responsibility for our actions at a young age. Therein lies the problem. I won't get into the semantics of proper parenting but there is a definite correlation between telling lies and getting punished.

Honesty is also difficult when we are ashamed of the truth. When we think our own behavior is shameful and yet cannot bring ourselves to stop it is hard to admit our mistake. How many people do you know who are completely open about their alcoholism or other addictions? We deny it. We want ourselves to be more perfect than we are. We want others to believe we are better than we are. That's human nature. Sometimes this stems from pride but it also comes from shame. Should we come clean and admit all of our mistakes? Probably not. Personal problems are difficult to solve and "help" from others can often be detrimental. Besides, if we cultivate a culture in which everyone always admits to all of their mistakes, the temptation will be to judge others for their mistakes and to take it upon ourselves to correct them. I don't really want seven billion people telling me how to live my life better.

Being honest is sometimes difficult. It requires strength and courage to take responsibility for our actions. Therein lies the need for great self-control. If we are honest with others, we do not deceive. We've already talked about the kind of destruction falsehood can bring. Let's talk about how honesty nurtures our society.

Have you ever admired someone for owning up to their mistakes? It's an admirable quality to be sure. When we are honest with others we encourage them to be honest with us. It relates to the fear of punishment. If we slowly learn that we won't be chastised, berated and ridiculed for making mistakes but rather be lauded for our honesty it becomes easier to be honest. And perhaps when people realize that we are trying to be honest and own up to our mistakes they will be less likely to chastise and ridicule. Taking responsibility is a virtuous deed. Everyone makes mistakes but it takes honesty to breed an honest culture that celebrates responsibility. That is how honesty is a nurturing deed. Like energy begets energy, honesty begets honesty.

Honesty by itself is a good thing, but there are times when its exercise can be damaging to others. That's where a thing known as tact comes into play. In order for us to be altruistically honest we must also devote ourselves to tactfulness. Have you ever spoken the truth about something and others have gotten upset? Chances are it is because you were pointing out someone's shortcomings in a public setting or because you were speaking the truth in a demeaning way. Imagine, if you will, that someone has an atrocious hairdo that they feel looks completely awesome and they ask you what your opinion is of that hairdo whilst among a group of their friends. The truth is that, in your opinion, the hairdo is atrocious. If we approach this situation without tact, though we are honest, we can severely hurt that person's feelings. We might say exactly what we think of the hairdo, making a fool of that person in front of their friends. We might say that the hairdo looks atrocious which sounds pretty bad from our friend's perspective. Now, let's say we approach the same situation with tact. We pull our friend aside where others cannot hear so that they don't look like a fool. Instead of saying that it looks atrocious, we instead say that we don't think it looks very good or that it doesn't compliment our friends looks. Now that we've done that, the truth has been spoken but feelings are much less likely to get hurt. Our friend may even thank us for being honest and they will certainly be glad we didn't point out the bad hairdo in front of their friends. This is the exercise of tact. One of the great flaws of us as a people is that we say what we believe to be true with severity and malice and then justify our lack of tact with the expression "it's okay because it's the truth." This kind of honesty might help us be truthful but it does not cultivate a culture in which truth is appreciated.

    There's that saying from the Hindu culture again: Speak what is pleasant, speak what is true, but never speak an unpleasant truth.

    Honesty is an important part of a productive society because we cannot function efficiently if we are misinformed and do not understand the truth. In order to nurture a truthful society, tact is necessary.

The last important piece of honesty is the distinction between opinion and truth. We have a tendency to have high value of our own opinions. This tends to stem from our own pride and self-worth. However, very rarely do we acknowledge what is actually truth and what is merely our opinion. For example, what is beautiful to one is not necessarily to another, so beauty is more opinion than it is truth.

"Gibbons mate with gibbons. Deer mingle with deer. Mudsuckers carouse with mudsuckers. Humans consider Lady Feather and Deer-Grace the most beautiful of women. But if fish saw them, they'd head for deep water. If birds saw them, they'd scatter into azure depths. If deer saw them, they'd go bounding away. So of these four, which knows the truth about beauty for all beneath heaven."
(Chuang Tzu 28)

That's one reason it's a good idea to preface our opinions with "I think" or "in my opinion" and to end such statements with "but I could be wrong" or "but that's just me". That is also why we should never say "It's not an opinion, it's a fact." This is how to be gentle with one another.

Honesty can nurture great productivity within others as it allows them to operate with understanding. It can encourage others to be honest and to take responsibility for their actions. Honesty can correct problems. It is altruistic when it possesses tact and it can be harmful when it is tactless.

Empathy

Empathy is the psychological identification with or

vicarious experiencing of the feelings, thoughts, or attitudes of another.(Dictionary.com Empathy)

Another way of saying this is "empathy is seeing ourselves in others". While caring about others is certainly a virtue, empathy is altruistic because it is an act of identification with others that allows us great introspection and enables kindness, respect and consideration for the feelings of others. What distinguishes it from caring is the process of identification. Caring is a concern for someone or something. Empathy is the identification with someone or something. Empathy can generate concern but concern is not identification.

So why is identification so important? Recognizing ourselves in others corresponds to one of Jesus' great teachings: "Love others as you love yourself." (International Bible, MAT, 22:39) While in a simple way we should care about others, this teaching is far deeper than many of us realize. Remember how human nature tends to be concerned with the self? When we recognize our self in others we are also concerned with others. When we identify the pain in our self as the same pain in others we suddenly become conscientious of how our actions affect others. When we identify with the frustration, the compassion, the struggle and the shortcomings in others we recognize our own frustrations, compassion, struggles and shortcomings. Empathy allows us to hold up a mirror to ourselves and to act in a nurturing way with those who are making mistakes and struggling through life and it allows us to be respectful of others.

Jesus also spoke of loving our enemies. (International Bible, MAT, 5:44)

Surely you have acquaintances that you do not like or would prefer not to be around. We may never fully like someone but if we can identify with those we do not like we can act in ways that transform others from enemies into allies. Remember: an enemy is just a friend we haven't met yet. If we can empathize, we can truly meet our enemies. We have to learn to be compassionate and we have to learn to overcome our own ignorance and shortcomings to be empathetic. So too do our enemies. Not everyone is as developed as we are and we are not as developed as everyone either. If we hate others and act out in aggression toward others instead of being empathetic, we only encourage aggression in others. If we are empathetic, we encourage others to understand us as well.

The bigot is not empathetic. They may think they that they are. They may feel that they understand where others are coming from. However, bigots do not identify with the feelings, thoughts and attitudes of others. They stubbornly act against them. If a bigot were to identify with other beliefs, feelings and attitudes, they would recognize the pain they are causing others as the same pain they experience. If that were to happen, most likely the bigot would forgo bigotry and become tolerant and respectful to others. Humans typically try to avoid pain. If we are empathetic we try to diminish the pain of others.

"Love your enemies." (International Bible, MAT, 5:44) Enemies are just friends we haven't met yet. Empathy nurtures respect, growth, compassion, mercy, humbleness and understanding. It erases bigotry, apathy and pride. A community cannot thrive without empathy.

Goodwill

Lastly is goodwill. Goodwill is the desire to do good to others. Where empathy is identification with others, goodwill is the desire for the benefit of others. In a way, altruism and goodwill are the same. They both are involved with the welfare of others. We differentiate between the two because the welfare of others may not simply be a desire to do good, but perhaps the desire to relieve suffering. To clarify the differentiation, let's think in terms of envious behavior. Where envy is a feeling of discontent or covetousness with regards to another's advantages, success, possessions and so forth, goodwill is a desire for others to have those successes, possessions and advantages.

There is often a mentality of win-lose in society. We set ourselves up in competition with others. We want to beat our competition. We believe that if we are winning, someone else is losing, and if someone else is winning we believe that we are losing. This paradigm places us in a world of competitive selection. That is, those who win go on and those who lose are left behind. This kind of mentality places us in a divided world. If half continue and half are left behind in an endless series of competition much like the brackets of a tournament, over time we end up with only one champion. So, one champion wins and everyone else is left behind...? That doesn't sound like a thriving society to me. Instead, if we live in a win-win society, where everyone works for the mutual benefit of all, we would end up with a society where everyone thrives. While competition does push us to succeed through adversity, if we always live life like that we work solely for our own benefit and not the benefit of others. This leads to selfishness which leads to the myriad consequences we've already discussed. However, If the only person you compete against is yourself, you cannot help but to grow. Just because someone else succeeds does not mean that we do not succeed. Win-win mentality is the belief that there is more than enough to go around. Why should we not be happy when other good people have good things happen to them? Do we not want our children to thrive? Do we not desire good health for those we love? Without empathy, goodwill cannot flourish. Without goodwill we live in a win-lose or lose-lose world with envy and jealousy as our bosom companions. Goodwill is the only resistance to envy. (Covey 217-224)

As an act, because altruistic behaviors are both beliefs and practices, goodwill is expressed through the celebration of the achievements of others as well as the support of others to help them succeed. If you've ever been interested in dating someone and found out that they are already in a relationship with someone else, have you ever taken the time to be happy for them that they've found someone who makes them happy? Did you ever tell them that you were glad they have someone? That is altruistic. Have you ever applied for a job and known the other candidates? Were you happy for the one who got the job when you didn't? It is okay to want to have something, but we cannot forget to be glad for others who got such a thing. Doing so nurtures a win-win society instead of pitting us against one another in The Grand Tournament.

As mentioned before, bigotry lacks empathy. If empathy is necessary for goodwill, then bigotry does not possess goodwill. A bigot may have good intentions but not good will. Intention is a desired outcome. Goodwill is a desire for good things for others, not ourselves. A bigot is concerned with their own viewpoint which they feel is good from their perspective, albeit to the detriment of others from differing viewpoints.

While there are many beneficial virtues, in order for an act to be altruistic it needs to nurture society not merely be present within it. Self-control, charity, courage, industry, honesty, empathy and goodwill are acts that nurture society because they encourage good behavior and take care of others. When we can recognize these behaviors in others we are allowing ourselves to see the good in others. Even if those others are our enemies, altruistic behavior provides a solid foundation to bridge the gaps between differing cultures, beliefs and opinions. Remember: enemies are just friends we haven't met yet. Through understanding, we can erase bigotry and foster a culture that seeks truth and supports itself instead of tearing itself apart.

Neither Good or Evil

For Everything There Is A Season
    King Solomon said it best:
    "There is a time for everything, and a season for every activity under heaven:
    A time to be born and a time to die,
    a time to plant and a time to uproot,
    a time to kill and a time to heal,
    a time to tear down and a time to build,
    a time to weep and a time to laugh,
    a time to mourn and a time to dance,
    a time to scatter stones and a time to gather them,
    a time to embrace and a time to refrain,
    a time to search and a time to give up,
    a time to keep and a time to throw away,
    a time to tear and a time to mend,
    a time to be silent and a time to speak,
    a time to love and a time to hate,
    a time for war and a time for peace.
    I have observed the task which God has given the sons of man to be concerned with: He made everything beautiful in its time; He has also put an enigma into their minds so that man cannot comprehend what God has done from beginning to end.
    Thus I perceived that there is nothing better for them than to rejoice and do good in this life. Indeed every man who eats and drinks and finds satisfaction in all his labor – this is a gift of God.
    I realized that whatever God does will endure forever: Nothing can be added to it and nothing can be subtracted from it, and God has acted so that [man] should stand in awe of Him.

What has been, already exists, and what is still to be, has already been, and God always seeks the pursuers.

Furthermore, I have observed beneath the sun: In the place of justice there is wickedness, and in the place of righteousness there is wickedness. I mused: God will judge the righteous and the wicked, for there is a time for everything and for every deed, there.

Then I said to myself concerning men: 'God has chosen them, but only to see that they themselves are beasts.' For the fate of men and the fate of beast – they have one and the same fate: as one dies, so dies the other, and they all have the same spirit. Man has no superiority over beast, for all is futile.

All go to the same place; all originate from dust and all return to dust. Who perceives that the spirit of man is the one that ascends on high while the spirit of the beast is the one that descends down into the earth? I therefore observed that there is nothing better for man than to be happy in what he is doing, for that is his lot. For who can enable him to see what will be after him?"

(Stone Edition Chumash, Ecclesiastes 3)

If we are to truly develop as an intelligent society and serve the greater good, we have to acknowledge the benefit of all things, including things that may seem bad but are not inherently evil, such as death and disease, as well as things that seem good but are not inherently good. King Solomon knew well that everything happens. It is how we strive to understand everything that happens that makes us wise or foolish. Everything has its time. Those who are foolish tend to do things when it is not the right time.

Now that we've discussed things that are good and things that are bad, let's mix it up a bit. Consider this: There is no such thing as an absolute good. Many of the things humanity considers good or bad aren't just one way or the other. I've included this section in order to point out the fallacy of declaring an emotional state as solely good or solely evil. I've heard it said that "love is the answer", which seems to be built out of blind following and repetition. If we look at love, hate, anger, joy, hope and despair as they are, instead of some sort of absolute good or absolute evil, we can see the truth of those things and how they play into the greater picture.

All of these things are emotions. Emotions are like information. When we feel something it is in response to our environment, much like the physical sensation of pain or pleasure. When something is disgusting, we get disgusted. When we care for someone, we feel love and compassion. When things aren't going our way we get angry or sad. However, information and action are two very different things. Thus, when we receive information, it is what we choose to do with that information that determines whether or not we are doing something good.

Love

So what of love? Is love an absolute good? By itself, it is necessary. Humanity has proven through the ages that it has a difficult time living in a world without love. It is good to love and to be loved. However, love is not an absolute good. Humans have done horrific things in the name of love. Does love cause us to commit evil? By itself, love does not harm others, nor does it harm us. Love is an emotion. It is what we choose to do for love that can cause destruction. We make the choice to commit betrayal, violence and so forth. The evil does not come from love, from the emotion. It comes from the choice, from the mind.

For example, a man in his youth falls in love with a beautiful woman. His love instills in him desire to be with that woman. So he strives to prove himself worthwhile so that she will be impressed with him. He focuses on his self and puts others down. He tries to make everyone else look worse than himself so that by comparison he is the best option in the room. His love causes him to harm others.

Love is an emotion. It is a profoundly tender, passionate affection for another person. (Dictionary.com Love)

Just because we care about someone does not mean that we act in a good fashion. Again, emotions are like information. We must choose to do the right thing with that information.

Jesus taught his disciples to "love thy neighbor as you love thyself". He was of course speaking of compassion, and he was right. If we cannot be compassionate toward others, especially our enemies, then we cannot live peacefully as a people. However, if we place the love of one person above the well being of others, we can be capable of great harm.

Often the ones we love the most are the ones we hurt the most. We tend to feel more open to expressing our feelings and thoughts with those we care about. Sometimes we forget to filter out our thoughts and opinions that do not help our relationships. You will never hear more heated arguments than those between families and lovers. Is the kind of behavior that leads to such hurtful arguments good? Certainly not. It is born of selfishness. So it is difficult to truly say that love is an absolute good.

People have stolen, lied and even killed in the name of love. Are these things good? Of course not. Love, by nature, is a compassionate attachment to another human. Love informs our actions but it does not determine them. When we become selfish in the name of our love, that is when we do the greatest harm. When we are selfless in love, that is when we forge the greatest relationships.

Love is neither good nor evil. It is merely a state of

mind and an expression of the soul.

Hate

I cannot even begin to imagine how many times I've heard or been told that hatred is the worst thing on the planet. Perhaps you have heard the same. So let's take an objective look at hate.

To hate is to dislike intensely or passionately. (Dictionary.com Hate) Like love, it is an emotional state. Surely, we are capable of harming those things we hate greatly. It is hatred, after all, that led to so much turmoil during the time of racial segregation in the United States. In that regard, hatred is surely a contributing factor to selfish destructive acts.

We should never hate, we should always love, right? That's the message I hear in this day and age. After all, love is the answer, isn't it? We should always love. We should love, and not hate things like murder, rape, bigotry, racism, lies and abuse, right?

Of course not.

Hatred, applied to a person, group of people, or faith or belief, is the pathway to ignorance and destruction. In this sense, hatred is a terrible thing. However, hatred applied to terrible things is the driving factor in the quest for a better world. If I did not have such a strong hatred of bigotry and religious ignorance I would not be writing this book. If you did not hate terrible action, it would be much harder for you to become the best person you can be and encourage others to be the best they can be. Hatred is capable of causing harm when we are selfish, and capable of spurning us onward when we are selfless.

Consider things this way: God made us able to hate for a reason. Perhaps that reason is to help eliminate the poor behaviors humanity performs when we are selfish.

Though many may contend it, hatred is neither good

nor evil. It is merely a state of mind and an expression of the soul.

Jesus said "love thy neighbor as thyself". Solomon said "a time to love and a time to hate". We have to remember context when acknowledging these two seemingly different viewpoints. Jesus was speaking during a time where hatred was rampant and compassion was sorely needed in society. Solomon was speaking about the nature of existence. Both of them were right.

Anger

People become angry when the things they want or the situations they are in fail to meet their desires. So is anger evil? Just like hatred, it can spurn us on to do good. Selfishly, it can cause great harm, selflessly it motivates.

Anger is a strong feeling of displeasure aroused by a wrong. (Dictionary.com Anger)

Most people tend to get angry when things don't go their way. It's a fairly simple mechanic. Again, anger is an emotion. It is what we choose to do with it that can make it a good or bad thing.

As an example, a man I worked with was stressed out during an accident in our place of work and acted very resentfully toward me because I did not personally handle the situation. He didn't know that I was incapable of resolving the situation. He grew hostile toward me. It made me mad. I couldn't help in that moment that I was incapable. To say the least, things were not going my way. However, instead of lashing out at him, I used my anger to exact the most perfect revenge. My vengeance was to be the bigger man. I chose instead to resolve the issue by educating myself about the accident and how to deal with it. I made amends with him. Anger became a fuel for me to be the best person I could be. I used it to provide energy and used my mind instead of my emotions to deal with the issue at hand. A true faith is not preached, it is lived. It is taught to others through action, not rhetoric.

Anger tends to get the adrenaline pumping, which provides the body with a boost of energy. If we embrace the anger and satisfy it, we tend to hurt others. If we can use up the energy before we hurt others, at least we won't be so likely to cause harm. Even better, if we can use the energy in an intelligent fashion, we can do great good.

Anger is an emotion. It is neither good nor evil. It is merely a state of mind and an expression of the soul.

Joy

Let's look at the definition of joy. Joy is the emotion of great delight or happiness caused by something exceptionally good or satisfying; keen pleasure or elation. (Dictionary.com Joy)

Sounds pretty good doesn't it? So let's see if we can find an example of joy that is not good.

Can joy be found in causing harm to others? There's a term called sadism and it is exactly that. Sadism is joy derived by inflicting pain on others. The same can be said of masochism; Joy in causing harm to the self.

Joy is an emotion that we feel based on our desires. People are filled with joy when the things they want or the situations they are in successfully meet or exceed their desires. It can be the result of terrible selfish deeds or wholesome selfless action.

Joy is neither good nor evil. It is merely a state of mind and an expression of the soul. One can find great joy in the love of God. That is the purest essence of joy.

Hope

Hope is in some ways necessary. That is a simple truth. Without hope, people tend to be unmotivated to change the situations they find themselves in. Hope keeps us from committing suicide in the face of great despair. Without hope, the Jews may have perished long before the birth of Jesus Christ. It is good to have some semblance of hope.

Hope means to look forward to with desire and reasonable confidence. (Dictionary.com Hope)

Hope is hollow. It is a reflection of desire, not reality. Much like fear, hope is a feeling that concerns what might be but has not yet been realized.

So how can hope be less than good? Hope can keep us hoping instead of acting to change our situations. When we hope too strongly, we do not act. We wish for impossible things to happen. We hope that God will intervene and take away all of our suffering and solve all of our problems so we won't have to lift a finger. Sound a little like laziness, doesn't it? Humans are endlessly capable of rising to overcome great challenges, so long as we have at least some hope. However, when we are completely filled with hope we have no room for action and instead have unrealistic expectations.

Hope can both help and hinder us. It is neither good nor evil. It is merely a state of mind and an expression of the soul.

Despair

Despair is defined as the loss of hope. (Dictionary.com Despair) When people have no hope, they give up. They call it a day. They do not strive to overcome their obstacles in spite of the fact that humans are endlessly capable. If you want to see despair in its purest form, find someone who is suicidal. That is the greatest expression of despair. When we are filled with despair, we can be just as inactive as when we are filled with hope. Why bother doing anything when we know we are going to fail, right?

Despair is difficult to identify as more than just a bad thing unless we acknowledge its subtleties. When we lose hope (by gaining despair) when we are completely filled with hope, we begin to see reality more clearly. If a person is in the greatest heights of hope, despair brings them back to a neutral level. However, when we despair too much we lose sight of reality once again. There is a window between pure hope and pure despair through which the world becomes clear and simple truths can be recognized. Without despair to bring us down from being too hopeful, we cannot see clearly. With too much despair, we sink below reason and cannot see clearly.

Despair is both the stark reality to hope as well the blindness of inaction. If we cannot act because we are consumed with despair, no good can be done. Despair is neither good nor evil. It is merely a state of mind and an expression of the soul.

Death

Lastly, we have the subject of death. Every living creature on this planet becomes alive at one point or another and later, be it years or months or days, dies. We often fear death and the death of others for a variety of reasons. Some of the most common being an attachment to others or an attachment to our own lives. When someone we care for deeply dies, we may feel slighted or betrayed by our universe or our creator. We become vengeful against whatever caused that death. We grow fearful of those things that are deadly. Of course, the need for survival is inherent. We all want to survive and there is nothing wrong with that. However, there is no thing that will completely prevent the death of our mortal bodies. Even if a human could live in perfect health and thus be "immortal", perfect health does not guarantee forever life. One could never suffer an ailment and yet be killed by a natural disaster or another person's actions. So it is certain that we will die. One cannot avoid it.

"The mighty Mudball of a world burdens us with a body, troubles us with life, eases us with old age, and with death gives us rest. We call our life a blessing, so our death must be a blessing too."
(Chuang Tzu 60)

"Birth and death are certainly great events," replied Confucius. "But for him (the sage/cripple) they change nothing. All heaven and earth could be churned over and falling apart, but for him nothing would be lost. He inquires where nothing is false, and he isn't tossed about as things shift back and forth. He knows that the endless transformation of things unfurls according to its own inevitable nature, and he holds fast to the ancestral source."
(Chuang Tzu 49)

If death is inevitable then it cannot be perceived as intentional. It is natural. One cannot avoid it. It is destructive to life, that much is true. Certainly, when someone kills another person it is selfish and intentional, and in that sense becomes evil. However, by itself, without the intention of others but merely the unfurling of the universe it is not evil. It simply is the state in which our universe operates. If so, why should we fear it?

There are many things that some people consider to be either good or evil. If we seek to define and understand what those things are and what makes them good or evil instead of assuming that things are only one way or another, we can have a greater grasp of the truth. Emotions are not good or evil, they are emotions, and act like information to let us know how we should feel about a situation. Too often we hear that hate and despair and anger are bad and love and joy and hope are good. Delving into the nature of such things indicates that such is not necessarily true, though there may be a tendency with such things to be one way over another. The important point here is to acknowledge that many things are not just this or just that. There is a time for everything. A time to love and a time to hate.

The Important Question

There are so many unanswered questions people pose to gain some sort of deep understanding of existence and God and everything under the sun. Some questions try to give reason and purpose to our lives, others strive to explain the nature of existence. Where do we even start? Of the many I have heard, some of my favorites are: What is the meaning of life? Why are we here? What purpose do we serve? What should I do with my life? Is there a God? Why do we suffer?

These questions tend to rattle around in the brain and only occasionally do we decide upon an answer that we can live with. So far as I have seen, as a species, we haven't answered any of these questions fully and satisfactorily and the answers any one person has decided to be the truth are overly simple and tend to be unsatisfying to the rest of us. In short, we don't know the deeper meaning of the existence we are a part of.

It is clear, however, that we are searching. The fact that we continue to search for meaning is an encouraging sign. If we were to cease our search for truth the result would be an atrophy of the soul and the destruction of mankind. Without the search for meaning we feel purposeless. That search drives some into depression and a few even to suicide. Others it instills with joy and hope, and some with excitement and fervor. Humans need to feel that they have a point or a purpose. Without it we have a hard time functioning. That is one of the reasons faith is so important. Faith helps us continue on with our unanswered questions. So why, if faith is so important, do so many people neglect their own faith? Why do so many people fail to develop themselves and search for truth and instead accept a simple answer handed out by someone else that may or may not be the truth?

    One important question we ought to ask is this: Is the neglect of our search for truth and the lack of development of our faith the reason that humanity falls prey to its own self destruction?

    Here is a simple truth: You can believe what you want. You are fully capable. That is the nature of the world. With that in mind, do our beliefs serve humanity? Or does it only serve ourselves? In the end, what good will our beliefs bring about?

    If we believe that Lucifer's rebellion, according to theology, should be the example and that humanity should do whatever it wants to spite God and satisfy carnal desires, we have that capability. Does it benefit anyone? Or is it a selfish attempt to lash out at a world that has somehow wronged us? Is it selfish, destructive and intentional? Or can it serve the greater good?

    Another thing we might consider is where our faith is leading us. Does our faith leads to a world in which everyone would want to live? Can it bring about a utopia? What is the end game of our beliefs? At its greatest expression, what does the full realization of our faith look like? What are the consequences (and I mean all of the consequences)? One thing history has proven time and again is that the ends don't justify the means. Sacrificing the lives of millions of people does not justify the peace it might bring. When we do something like that we fall prey to the destruction of apathy toward the lives of our fellow human beings. While the world might change to some desired outcome, those who makes the choice to do great harm to obtain a desirable end are forever changed. Sacrificing the sanctity of the soul at the expense of others to achieve a great good is no good at all.

With so many questions, perhaps it would be best to look at just one. Let's take a look at just one of the great questions that tends to baffle us: Why are we here?
It is hard to believe that this questions can or will be answered by Science. Science may be able to answer the how, what, when and where we are here, but not the why. From a purely empirical standpoint reason is not found. In the face of creation it loses its place. All that is found is the physical cause. 'Why' is left to philosophy and faith.

As to the debate over the existence of God; At this time, we as humans do not have the means to imagine any form of proof that is not in some way observable to us in the physical realm. We seek to prove or disprove God and our only evidence is the world that we perceive which we have no means to view beyond. It seems rather silly that we should try to prove using a physical world something that exists perhaps beyond, around, within and without but not limited to the physical world. In short, it is a fool's quest. A goldfish cannot attempt to discern the center of the universe. It is limited to its fishy capacities and the water in which it lives. We cannot discern God through our feeble musings without the means to perceive beyond what we currently can perceive. Thus, we resort to our faith, which shapes our beliefs, and through those beliefs, shapes ourselves and our society.

Without God there is no reason for existence. If there is no reason, then why should we suffer?
"To find peace!" Some might say.

To what end do we seek peace?
"For happiness, of course."
And what does happiness accomplish?
"Progress", one might argue.
And what is the point of progress?
"Growth, surely."
And why do we need to grow?

    If there is a question that is worth asking in the context of theology, consider this one: if there truly is an entity such as God, why are we here at all? Are we necessary for existence, like our lungs are necessary for our bodies to live? If we were like the lungs of the body of existence, then we are necessary for the survival of existence, but we are far from in control. Are we like the mind of existence, and thus necessary and in control? Or are we more like a mole, unnecessary but nonetheless a part of the body? Are we here to prove a point? Are we here to serve God or are we merely a random byproduct? Many would contend that the universe will go on without humanity but humanity can surely not go on without the universe.

    There are some who believe that man was made in God's image. Perhaps this is true. I doubt that we physically look like God since God is so immense it would be impossible to make comparisons. However, perhaps in spirit and soul we are like God, much like pieces of clay are like the pot they make up. (Upanishads Vol 2 235) Monotheistically speaking, God is one and without a second. Is God lonely? Is God using us as an experiment to determine if God should make another God to keep God's self company? Perhaps God is simply a story teller telling out every possible story through this our cosmos for some unknowable reason. The possibilities are endless, and these are merely the simple and incomplete answers to large questions that will not satisfy everyone. The hope is that this writing will spurn the intellectual quest for truth and encourage us to consider possibilities outside of our current understanding, and through that create a greater tolerance for beliefs other than our own.

In Conclusion

What we seek is a simplistic faith built not on ideas and perceptions that change, but basic principles that do not change over time. Things in old religions become outdated and obsolete. A true faith does not. I hope that this book has given you food for thought. The bigotry inflaming the United States of America as well as other parts of this world is deplorable and the only way that we can change is through spiritual education and the development of faith. I also hope that if you have no affiliation with a specific religion and are seeking some form of spiritual shelter, that this book has provided you with a foundation to help you find one for yourself. I have no greater desire than the betterment of the world in which we live, and you are a part of that world. I hope you find a renewed, strengthened and refined faith that truly serves you and others well.

About the Author

I would like to start by saying I'm not the first one to think the things within these pages, and not the first to write them. Secondly, I am including a summary of myself not because I feel that I am important, but because if I was reading this work myself I would be wondering who wrote it and why in the world I should believe a word written in it.

I started this project in 2012 due to my hunger for a stronger faith. I was at one of the lowest points in my life and had started attending a church in a nearby community. Things were going great, I was part of the choir and I felt my faith grow back to a healthier state after years of neglect. One day I was sitting with the choir when I felt the sudden but clear feeling that the "spirit of God" had left the church I was attending. The building felt all at once hollow. I was singing with the choir and I suddenly felt ill, so I left to go home.

I started reading the Bible because there was a disconnect in the religion I was raised in and the beliefs of fellow Christians. The question "Was Jesus The Son of God, a Prophet, or God Himself?" was raised, and I needed an answer. I'd like to believe I was guided to seek it, due in part to events in my life. A day later I bought my first International Bible. I read it front to back to answer for myself whether or not I truly believed that Christ was God, that he was a servant of God, or if he was just a man with some awesome wisdom. I was truly surprised by my own conclusion after reading the Bible. Once I had finished my reading and answered my questions about what the Bible actually said and what Jesus said according to those scriptures, I had more questions about other faiths and beliefs.

Because of it, my questions grew, and so I reached outside of my spiritual education. I felt that since so many people follow different faiths there must be something to each of the faiths out there. So I read the Qu'ran. When I had finished, I had answers but I also had more questions. I read the Torah, the Book of Mormon, the Tao Te Ching and The Inner Chapters by Chuang Tsu, the Upanishads and the Three Pure Land Sutras. All the while I collected notes of philosophies and notions each religion brought to bear in the hope that somewhere, somehow I would be able to determine what I truly believed that I might be able to live a good life and do good things with myself.

What I found were good teachings that, in spite of my religious upbringing, I had never been taught. Each of them (for the most part) contained wisdom inherent in all the books of various religions, and each of them possessed kernels of wisdom not possessed by the others. To me it was like the allegory of the blind men and the elephant. If I was truly going to gain an understanding of the elephant, I needed the input of all the blind men.

I was frustrated that there was no apparent religion in which I could seek shelter that did not appear ignorant or superstitious in some way. When I had finished my reading I began investing my time and energy into this writing, to simplify the fruits of my journey, so that I could share them with others. The goal was to give people who are as lost as I was a place to start thinking about faith without fear of judgment or indoctrination, free from the influence of ignorant minds and bigotry. In other words, a faith that made sense built on a solid foundation. From that foundation I hope that people will develop their own faiths to improve this our world. I'm sick of living in a world where bigotry is everywhere and people are more concerned with themselves and their appetites than with the welfare of all. The only way to cure that illness is to treat it at the source. The source is the spiritual education of every man, woman and child.

My life until then had been spent growing up, graduating from high school, trying to find a place in the world and be different and unique, cool and desirable and be better than everyone else. I realized in my search that I was a selfish person. Perhaps not completely, but enough that I needed to change. I believe that my search for faith has helped me grow into a better person and I hope to continue growing until my last breath. I don't regret beginning my search and in truth I doubt completely that the search will ever have an end.

I truly believe a person lost in their faith should read what I have read to stimulate thought and develop their faith on their own, but as I have written in the section titled The Path, people want to have an answer and live their lives with as little effort as possible. It took me three years to finish reading what I had read. Not everyone is willing to take the time to invest that much into their own faith (how unfortunate). The next best thing to investing years into reading is to use what I have gained and shared here to encourage free thought and help others develop themselves in the hopes that what I write will help erase the ignorance, bigotry and stubbornness that plague many religious circles. If you don't believe everything that I write, great! At least you will know what you don't believe. If you gain anything from this book, it is my fervent hope beyond all hopes that you have gained a distaste for bigotry and will strive to erase it from yourself and encourage others to do the same. That is the greatest reason I write this work.

In the short span I have been alive, I have seen no evidence to support that God demands of his followers to believe in past events which may or may not have occurred as they have been told through the generations. Nor have I seen evidence that blindly following any faith is a worthy endeavor. God does not seem to demand that his followers believe in the teachings of other men, nor in events that happened long before their time. To me, God's instructions have been laid out plain as day, and when we truly pay attention and stop acting selfishly, we begin to see those instructions. It is one thing to have faith that what people tell you is true. It is another entirely to have faith in God and to let him guide you through the world God has created.

I believe that evil is self-evident by the destruction it creates and that its source is our own selfish hearts.

It does not matter to me if readers believe that the history as portrayed in The Holy Bible or the Qu'ran or any holy book are true events (events that actually took place) without any other substitute. It is our faith in God and the lessons learned through stories and experience that matter. I would rather a person acted truly good in a search for truth then act terribly by assuming that they've already found it. A fictional story can still possess a good moral. A true story can be void of one. If we have faith that, regardless of fact or fiction, we can discern for ourselves right and wrong, so long as we allow God to guide us to the right path, then there is no end to the good we can do.

Sources

Carnegie, Dale. How to Win Friends and Influence People. New York, NY: Gallery Books, 1936.

Carnes, Patrick J. and Adams, Kenneth M. Clinical Management of Sex Addiction. Taylor & Francis Books, 2002.

Carroll, Lewis. Alice's Adventures in Wonderland & Other Stories. 2010 edition.
Comp. Barnes & Noble. New York: Barnes & Noble 1994.

Chuang Tzu. Chuang Tzu: The Inner Chapters. Translated by David Hinton. Berkeley, CA: Counterpoint, 2014.

Covey, Stephen R. The 7 Habits of Highly Effective People. New York: Simon & Schuster, 2004. Nov 2013 Edition.

"Altruism." Def 1. Dictionary.com. 2016, www.dictionary.com. Accessed 9 October, 2016.

"Anger." Def 1. Dictionary.com. 2016, www.dictionary.com. Accessed 9 October, 2016.

"Bigot." Def 1. Dictionary.com. 2016, www.dictionary.com. Accessed 9 October, 2016.

"Bigotry." Def 1. Dictionary.com. 2016, www.dictionary.com. Accessed 9 October, 2016.

"Charitable." Def 1. Dictionary.com. 2016, www.dictionary.com. Accessed 9 October, 2016.

"Confidence." Def 2. Dictionary.com. 2016, www.dictionary.com. Accessed 9 October, 2016.

"Despair." Def 1. Dictionary.com. 2016, www.dictionary.com. Accessed 9 October, 2016.

"Destroy." Def 1. Dictionary.com. 2016, www.dictionary.com. Accessed 9 October, 2016.

"Empathy." Def 1. Dictionary.com. 2016, www.dictionary.com. Accessed 9 October, 2016.

"Envy." Def 1. Dictionary.com. 2016, www.dictionary.com. Accessed 9 October, 2016.

"Fate." Def 3. Dictionary.com. 2016, www.dictionary.com. Accessed 9 October, 2016.

"Fear." Def 1. Dictionary.com. 2016, www.dictionary.com. Accessed 9 October, 2016.

"Gluttony" Def 1. Dictionary.com. 2016, www.dictionary.com. Accessed 9 October, 2016.

"Hate." Def 1. Dictionary.com. 2016, www.dictionary.com. Accessed 9 October, 2016.

"Hope." Def 6. Dictionary.com. 2016, www.dictionary.com. Accessed 9 October, 2016.

"Jealousy." Def 2. Dictionary.com. 2016, www.dictionary.com. Accessed 9 October, 2016.

"Joy." Def 1. Dictionary.com. 2016, www.dictionary.com. Accessed 9 October, 2016.

"Love." Def 1. Dictionary.com. 2016, www.dictionary.com. Accessed 9 October, 2016.

"Lust." Def 2. Dictionary.com. 2016, www.dictionary.com. Accessed 9 October, 2016.

"Morality." Def 1. Dictionary.com. 2016, www.dictionary.com. Accessed 9 October, 2016.

"Panic." Def 1. Dictionary.com. 2016, www.dictionary.com. Accessed 9 October, 2016.

"Preach." Def 1-6. Dictionary.com. 2016, www.dictionary.com. Accessed 9 October, 2016.

"Preacher." Def 1. Dictionary.com. 2016, www.dictionary.com. Accessed 9 October, 2016.

"Pride." Def 1. Dictionary.com. 2016, www.dictionary.com. Accessed 9 October, 2016.

"Priest." Def 1, 2. Dictionary.com. 2016, www.dictionary.com. Accessed 9 October, 2016.

"Religion." Def 1, 2. Dictionary.com. 2016, www.dictionary.com. Accessed 9 October, 2016.

"Sloth." Def 1. Dictionary.com. 2016, www.dictionary.com. Accessed 9 October, 2016.

"Virtue." Def 5. Dictionary.com. 2016, www.dictionary.com. Accessed 9 October, 2016.

The Holy Bible, New International Version. Cincinnati: Zondervan House, 1984. Print.

The Holy Qu'ran. With English Translation and Commentary by Maulana Muhammad Ali. 2002 edition. Ohio: Ahmadiyya Anjuman Isha 'at Islam Lahore Inc., 2002.

Kyokai, Bukkyo Dendo. BDK English Tripitaka: The Three Pure Land Sutras. Translated by Inagaki Hisao. Berkeley, CA: Numata Center for Buddhist Translation and Research, 2003.

Lao-Tzu. Tao Te Ching. Translated by Stephen Mitchell. London: Kyle Books, 1988.

Nikhilananda, Swami. The Upanishads Volume 1, Sixth Edition. New York, NY: Ramakrishna-Vivekananda Center, 2003.

Nikhilananda, Swami. The Upanishads Volume 2, Sixth Edition. New York, NY: Ramakrishna-Vivekananda Center, 2004.

Nikhilananda, Swami. The Upanishads Volume 3, Sixth Edition. New York, NY: Ramakrishna-Vivekananda Center, 2007.

Nikhilananda, Swami. The Upanishads Volume 4, Sixth Edition. New York, NY: Ramakrishna-Vivekananda Center, 2008.

Nicks, Denver. "The U.S. Is Becoming Less Religious, Survey Shows." Time Magazine. November 3rd, 2015.

"Physical Health and Mental Health." Mental Health Foundation. Mental Health Foundation, March 5th, 2017. Accessed March 5th, 2017. https://www.mentalhealth.org.uk/a-to-z/p/physical-health-and-mental-health

Sherman, Rabbi Nosson. The Chumash. New York: Mesorah Publications, LTD, 2000.

Smith, Joseph. The Book of Mormon. First English edition published in 1830. Salt Lake city, Utah: The Church of Jesus Christ of Latter-day Saints, June, 1981.

Sun Tzu. The art of war. Filiquarian Publishing, LLC, 2015

www.ingramcontent.com/pod-product-compliance
Lightning Source LLC
Chambersburg PA
CBHW032036290426
44110CB00012B/831